Breaking the Sound Barrier

A Communication on Being Deaf

LOIS HOOPER DIAMOND
with BRIAN DIAMOND

Copyright © 2018 Lois Hooper Diamond.

All rights reserved. No part of this book may be reproduced, stored, or transmitted by any means—whether auditory, graphic, mechanical, or electronic—without written permission of the author, except in the case of brief excerpts used in critical articles and reviews. Unauthorized reproduction of any part of this work is illegal and is punishable by law.

This book is a work of non-fiction. Unless otherwise noted, the author and the publisher make no explicit guarantees as to the accuracy of the information contained in this book and in some cases, names of people and places have been altered to protect their privacy.

ISBN: 978-1-4834-7832-6 (sc)
ISBN: 978-1-4834-7833-3 (e)

Library of Congress Control Number: 2017919065

Because of the dynamic nature of the Internet, any web addresses or links contained in this book may have changed since publication and may no longer be valid. The views expressed in this work are solely those of the author and do not necessarily reflect the views of the publisher, and the publisher hereby disclaims any responsibility for them.

Any people depicted in stock imagery provided by Thinkstock are models, and such images are being used for illustrative purposes only. Certain stock imagery © Thinkstock.

Lulu Publishing Services rev. date: 03/29/2018

This belongs to Marilyn McCallon

This book is dedicated to my family:

My father and mother who saw beyond my deafness and encouraged me to believe in myself; my brothers Donald, Melvin, Sterling, and Miles who always treated me as "one of the guys"; and my children, who inspired me to be the best that I can be.

Contents

Preface ix
Acknowledgement xxi

Part I: My introduction to the sound barrier

Chapter 1   My Early Years.. 1
Chapter 2   My New World.. 8

Part II: Some history and culture behind the sound barrier

Chapter 3   Meet the Hatfields and McCoys 21
Chapter 4   Deafness: hearing loss or a culture? 34

Part III: Life behind the sound barrier

Chapter 5   Living without sound... 45
Chapter 6   Missing Information 54

Part IV: Breaking the sound barrier: Interpreters, Technology, and Employment

Chapter 7   Sign Language Interpreters 67
Chapter 8   The Wonderful World of Technology............................. 77
Chapter 9   The Workplace... 93

Part V: Deaf children today: A future without a sound barrier

Chapter 10   Hearing Parents, Deaf Child..103

Afterword.. 125
References 127

Preface

For many years I have wanted to write this kind of book. Time and time again people have asked me questions about deafness. They would often ask me strange or difficult to explain questions about my own Deafness or about deaf/Deaf[1] people in general, and I had encountered many misunderstandings. I wanted to write a simple and clear book on a variety of issues. Over the years I kept a journal with the sole purpose that, when the time was right, I would write a book. Every person's story in this book is real, along with his or her viewpoints on those of us who do not hear. The anecdotes are from friends, associates, colleagues, clients, and deaf/Deaf people from all walks of life that I have encountered through the years.

Much of the information for this book began in 1975 when I moved to northern California from Los Angeles. My children and I moved to the lovely little town of Pollock Pines, 60 miles east of Sacramento. While we enjoyed living there, I became lonely after a while because there were no Deaf people anywhere close. I missed the enjoyment of communicating with my Deaf friends in American Sign Language (ASL). One day I journeyed into Sacramento to seek Deaf friends and check out the local college. To my surprise, the hearing people I met that signed were using Signed English (signs in English word order). At that point, I assumed that the Deaf in Sacramento did not use ASL, our native and natural language. However, when I went to check out a local bowling alley where several Deaf people congregated, I was relieved to see that all of them used ASL. In a conversation with an old Deaf friend whom I knew from my days at the Berkeley School for the Deaf, I mentioned how I was surprised that the local college taught a way of signing that the native Deaf did not use.

---

[1] The distinction between deaf/Deaf is explained in Chapter 4

He said parents with deaf children were taught to use that different way of signing. I asked if there were any Deaf leaders in Sacramento that I could meet and discuss this with. He mentioned a Judy Tingley (now Viera), a Deaf teacher who taught at a local high school.

As soon as I had the opportunity, I drove down from the hills to seek out this woman. Judy was a refined middle-aged woman of high education. I was immediately taken by her intelligence. Being an established teacher of deaf children, she had connections with parents and other schools. I told her about how surprised I was that hearing people in Sacramento who signed did not use ASL. I also told her that I was enrolled in American River College and was the only Deaf student there. I explained to Judy that it felt strange being the only Deaf student, but that I enjoyed working with my interpreter, Alvin Roth. Alvin was one of only a handful of interpreters in Sacramento at the time. He used ASL, as he had Deaf parents. Most of the interpreters back in 1975 were children of Deaf parents. I asked Judy if there was anything I could do to teach people learning sign to be taught our natural language. She said to let her think on this and she would get back to me.

A short time later, Judy contacted me and informed me that she had set up a meeting with some parents of deaf children and the President of Sacramento City College (SCC) and she wanted me to attend this meeting. When we all met in the conference room, I was kind of scared. I did not have any experience in these kinds of meetings. So, I sat silently watching as the parents and Judy argued that we needed an ASL class so we could have more interpreters for our deaf children. The President seemed bored and resistant, and kept saying there was no funding. He claimed he had too many elective classes, such as macramé to be able to meet our wants. After about an hour, Judy turned to me and said, "Speak up for yourself!" My legs began to tremble, but I started this, so I thought I had better say something. I stood up, and via the ASL interpreter, said to the President, "I appreciate your time with us. I have sat here for an hour listening to your excuses about not having enough money to set up an ASL class. But let me tell you, we need an ASL class. I want an education. Many Deaf people want an education. Many of us want to get off Welfare or Social Security and go to work. Deaf children need an education. They will have this opportunity when sufficient interpreters are available. If you really wanted to help us, you would cut out those useless macramé classes and use the money for the Deaf, who, like me, want to be independent." I sat down to a shocked room full of stares. I thought, *"How stupid of me to speak out so direct! I probably embarrassed everyone."* When everyone got up to leave, I lagged behind, talking to the interpreter. The President stopped and told the interpreter "Tell her that I appreciated her honesty in the meeting and that I like her." Trying to be funny and keep it light, I told the interpreter, "Tell him I like him too. But I would like him more if he would set up an ASL class." His eyes got big and shiny, and to my surprise, he reached out and kissed me on the cheek.

One week later Judy informed me that SCC agreed to have an ASL class! Then she asked if I would become the ASL Instructor. *"But I would need an interpreter to help with the classes,"* I griped (again, we had almost none back then). She told me she had already thought of that. There was a young girl named Sandy Canada who was hard of hearing and used ASL. She could hear well enough to help us get by. I said, "Yes, let's give it a try."

The year was 1976. Back in those days, there were no structured sign language classes like today. So, I went to the bookstore and the library, checked out the best sign language books, and designed the classes as I thought they should be taught: beginning with finger spelling, then colors and shapes, animals' signs, family signs, and then onto simple sentences. There was so much interest in the classes that they grew faster than expected. After one year, I had to find another ASL teacher to take on a class!

While teaching, I was also working part-time at the Resources for Independent Living (RIL). It was the only service center for the disabled at the time. Judy, seeing the need for a service center for the Deaf, submitted a grant proposal. With the support of the Deaf community leaders and parents of deaf children, NorCal Center on Deafness (NorCal) was established. The first Executive Director for NorCal was Willis Mann, an intelligent Deaf leader with past experience working at the National Association for the Deaf (NAD) in Maryland. When I met Willis, he asked me to work for NorCal as a Community Education Specialist. The job would be to educate people of the Sacramento community, who can hear, about deafness. Unfortunately, due to my lack of experience, the Board denied my application. It was two years until I was hired for this position, with Mr. Mann telling the Board that he would personally be responsible for seeing that I got a lot of professional training and mentoring.

True to his word, Mr. Mann sent me all over for professional training. I went to the University of Maryland to learn how to train hospitals on the care of deaf patients. Upon returning, I went to local hospitals and trained their staff. I then went to Arizona for training on Deaf leadership. Following that, I spent two weeks at Gallaudet University, then back to the University of Arizona for more training. Many other training opportunities followed.

As the Community Education Specialist, I put out a "needs assessment" for the local Deaf citizens; it seemed their main interest was to have Deaf social events. We began fundraisers to bring the Sacramento Deaf Community together. We then had a party with a live band (if you are wondering how the Deaf enjoy a live band, keep in mind all deaf persons are not 100% deaf. Some have moderate hearing, some are hard of hearing, and others who are totally deaf feel the vibrations on the wooden floor). We also started an annual Christmas Open House to get the Deaf community together and make the hearing public aware of our services at NorCal.

We got local TV talk shows to do stories about our service center, how to use a TTY (a teletype phone), and understand the importance of interpreters. At the time, the Railroad Museum in Old Sacramento (a major history attraction of Sacramento) had audio tours. We got them to add small print in the front of each train so deaf persons could read the railroad history. They also agreed to have captions added to their films. There were no signed or interpreted tours of the State Capitol, so we got a regular signing tour. We also got a TTY line installed and added the TTY number in brochures about the Capitol so the deaf/Deaf could call to set up a signed tour. Deaf children now had the opportunity to learn the history of the railroad, as well as the Capitol. In time, we had senators and assemblymen supporting our Deaf Awareness Month. They had a reception to let deaf kids meet their representatives.

During my tenure at NorCal, I realized that some of our Deaf clients needed mental health counseling. There had never been any such thing in Sacramento. Clearly, the deaf/Deaf people's needs had been overlooked. We also had some parents who could hear that needed help with their deaf children. I contacted the Department of Health Services (DHS) and brought to their attention that there was no counseling available for the deaf/Deaf in Sacramento. They were quite willing to work with me on this. They set up the Sacramento County Advisory Committee, who acted to give the Sacramento County Board of Supervisors information and guidance regarding lack of access for those with disabilities. I was asked to join the Advisory Committee—which I did for about four years. With the help of everyone in the group, were able to get a counselor for the Deaf and deaf-related issues at the local Mental Health Center.

My desire to make every program accessible for my Deaf peers in Sacramento became a "thirst" for me—having been denied so much access myself for so many years. My next project was the Sacramento Music Circus, a big tent where musical theatre performances took place. Having hearing before becoming deaf at the age of seven from spinal meningitis, I still had some interest in music. The singing and dancing at the Music Circus was enjoyable, however, it would have been more enjoyable for Deaf people if there were an interpreter present. I approached the manager about this, asking him to let us have an interpreter sign the performances. He agreed! This was covered in our local newspaper, the Sacramento Bee. We had volunteer interpreters for several years until the Americans with Disabilities Act (ADA) passed, and interpreters began being paid for their services.

We had a beautiful old museum in Sacramento called the Crocker Art Museum (now updated and modernized). I wanted to help some in the Deaf community further appreciate art, and thought a way to do so would be to have a Deaf docent give tours. A Deaf teacher at one of our local mainstream schools was interested. After a meeting with the Board at the museum, they agreed to train the teacher and begin monthly tours for Deaf adults and children.

With the growth of my job demands as the Community Education Specialist, I could no longer handle teaching sign language at SCC. I was working late many nights doing presentations for the Lion's and Rotary Clubs, planning picnics, fundraisers etc. I saw less and less of my children. I decided that one of my students, Patricia Schilling (now Masterson) would make a good replacement. I assured her that I would turn over all my materials and explain how to run the classes. My instinct was correct, because not only did she expand the ASL classes at SCC, she also worked with other colleges. I had set up a monthly coffee social across the street from SCC to get the students to interact with Deaf people, and I insisted that these socials be kept going. Today, there are Deaf coffee socials and pizza socials all over the Sacramento area, and ASL teachers have their students attend these socials that go on in Sacramento. Other cities throughout California copied this, and parts of the US have these types of Deaf socials today.

There is a former sign language student of mine that must be mentioned: Peggy Selover. She was in my class in 1977. I was always on the lookout for students who could possibly one day become interpreters. I had my eye on Peggy. One day she informed me that she was moving to Washington DC to get married. I was sad to lose her, but I encouraged her to visit Gallaudet University and continue her studies in ASL. She got involved in many efforts to empower the Deaf in the DC area, and ultimately became an advocate for Deaf rights.

It was an election year (1980), and Peggy submitted a proposal to the Presidential Campaign Committee of Ted Kennedy, which resulted in her becoming his (volunteer) National Coordinator of Services for the Deaf. She was successful in securing sign language interpreters for many of his campaign speeches around the country. This was a groundbreaking effort to include the Deaf Community more fully in the political realm. When it came time for the Democratic Convention in New York, Peggy coordinated interpreters to volunteer their services for the candidates. Deaf people across the nation were shocked (and of course happy) to see this type of interpreting for the first time ever. This was an historic event, and it was the beginning of interpreting and captioning seen at major political events today.

In 1985, Peggy moved back to California. She told me how she often wondered why American Sign Language was not offered as a foreign language at high schools. After all, American Sign Language is not English—it has own syntax and grammar. Therefore, sign language should be considered a foreign language like French or Spanish. Peggy began a grass roots effort to include ASL as a foreign language in high school curriculums. She and I discussed this effort, and I encouraged her to go the Deaf Community leaders first, seeking understanding of her efforts and support for the idea (language is culture, and ASL belongs to the Deaf culture). I explained that this effort could be seen as "the hearing world trying to take over the language of the Deaf." Peggy was determined that this would not happen. She connected with leaders in the Deaf communities throughout California, and explained in presentations that, if passed, the result of this legislation would be an opportunity of communication for the Deaf individuals in all parts of their lives. Some of the most respected leaders in the Deaf communities came on board as members of a committee to work with Peggy toward passage of the bill. Through the combined effort of many individuals, the bill (AB 51) was passed into law in 1986. American Sign Language was given full status as a foreign language within the California high school system. While the real intention of this bill was for high school students to take ASL as a foreign language in preparing them for college, Sacramento area colleges quickly began offering ASL classes in their Foreign Language departments. The idea spread to other cities in California, then into other states. Today ASL is offered in colleges in almost every state in America. However, Sacramento still has the largest number of sign language classes in the nation. Why shouldn't we? It all started right here.

I will never forget the day a hearing businessman by the name of Gary Upchurch walked into NorCal carrying a little box with him that looked like a typewriter. It was known as a telephone device for the deaf (TDD). This TDD was a smaller, streamlined version of the current mailbox sized TTY machines that many of us Deaf had at the time. After giving me a demonstration of how it worked and how it could benefit both the deaf and hearing to communicate, I was quite impressed. I took him into Mr. Mann's office, and Mr. Upchurch gave another demonstration. Mr. Mann was also quite amazed. He told me to take Mr. Upchurch to the California Association of the Deaf (CAD) office in downtown Sacramento to show it to the Executive Director, who became equally excited. The Executive Director proposed that lawmakers give TDD's to Deaf persons with their paid telephone service. Sometime later, Deaf leaders at CAD and other Deaf agencies in California got involved with this idea as well. I was not a part of that. However, I was asked to "round up all the Deaf people in Sacramento and get down to the Capitol" when the Legislature was considering a bill allowing deaf/Deaf persons to have free TDD's. I spent that entire day making calls, telling Deaf people to tell all their other Deaf friends about this. The next day, about 30 Deaf people showed up at the Capitol. We all crowded into a small room. When a Legislator saw so many deaf people, he asked, "How many of you are deaf and want a TDD?" We all raised our hands, and the process to pass the bill began immediately.

Following this exciting event, NorCal worked with the CAD and other Deaf service centers throughout California and announced that we would set up a "relay center." The relay center would have a few people who hear take calls on a TDD from a deaf person, and then voice the text to a hearing person who did not have a TDD. So, NorCal had one of the first (tiny) relay centers in the nation.

Before the ADA, Sacramento police would sometimes arrest Deaf males and then deprive them of their rights to contact a lawyer or have access to an interpreter. Because I became known in the Sacramento area as an advocate for Deaf rights, some of those who were arrested would call me for help. Sometimes, my sons answered the phone at 2:00 in the morning with a call from some hearing stranger asking me to pick up a Deaf person—who had asked the hearing stranger to make a telephone call for them. Again, this was years before the passage of the ADA. I set up a meeting with a police sergeant and an interpreter to discuss training and educating the police on dealing with Deaf inmates. I was met with resistance, but eventually the Sacramento Police Department received training on how to contact an interpreter 24 hours a day, install a TDD for Deaf inmates to call out, and on how to use a TDD when Deaf persons called the jail to inquire about a family member being detained.

That period in my life was a very rewarding experience. Before leaving NorCal, I received a "Woman of the Year" award from the local National Organization of Women (NOW) for my work in promoting the lives of Deaf women. I also received an "Honorary Recognition Award" from the California State Legislature for improving the quality of life for deaf people, and was nominated for the "Most Inspirational Disabled Person of Sacramento" by the Christian Berets. I am honored and grateful to have been able to work at NorCal, and fortunate to work with all the wonderful and talented people that I did.

After leaving NorCal, I got a job with the State of California Department of Health Services. I had an interesting experience interviewing for that job. Unfortunately, I could not set up an interpreter that day (again,

Sacramento did not have many interpreters back then). I decided to do the best I could by myself. Since I can speak and lip-read fairly well, I took a gamble. When I was led into the interview room, I was not nervous or scared. I knew I would be able to give them a good impression of myself. When we started the interview, I apologized for not having an interpreter, and told them I would do the best I could to communicate without one. The interviewers wanted to know if I had the ability to communicate with the public to get the needed supplies to all their offices. I explained my ability to deal with the public in person, as well as on a TDD. I informed them I would need a TDD to order office supplies and talk to the vendors and other office branches. I explained that all I would need more than a TDD, would be an interpreter for the staff meetings. I believe the interviewers were a bit surprised when they saw how independent I was and how I interacted with those who hear. They told me to wait in the lobby. Ten minutes later, they came out and asked if I could start on Monday.

In 1991, after the ADA was signed into law, I was surprised that many Deaf employees working for the State of California in Sacramento still did not have TDD access. There were some other Deaf employees who worked up the street in other State agencies, and we had weekly lunches together. During one of our luncheons, I brought up the fact that we did not have TDD's or have interpreters on the staff. From my research, the issue about the TDD's had been brought up to the State Personnel Board (SPB) in the past, but nothing materialized. I suggested that we work together and confront the SPB on these issues again. After several luncheon discussions, the Deaf employees agreed that we needed to call a meeting with the SPB. We needed to demand TDD access for all the deaf employees of the State of California, and we should request full time interpreters at State agencies that had many Deaf employees. My colleagues requested that I take the lead role in this, since I had experience with these types of issues. I called the SPB and requested an appointment with an interpreter present. Three other deaf/Deaf employees agreed to come with me. At this meeting, I was very direct, and told them that this issue had been brought up before and had been ignored. Abiding by the ADA should result in having TDD access and having more interpreters working for the State. As expected, there was some resistance. I ended the meeting by informing them that if they did not comply with the ADA, they would face a class action lawsuit.

A week later, we all had TDD's on our desks! Shortly after that, many State agencies began recruiting full time interpreters (today TTDs are outdated, and most employees use the latest phone technology, videophones, and the Video Relay Service known as "VRS.")

In 1994, two days before Thanksgiving, I suffered a mild heart attack. I did not feel good that morning when I woke up, but I had promised my son that I would drive the 30 miles to his house to have breakfast with him. However, once I arrived, I informed him that I was feeling terrible and had to return home. Driving home, I began to have shortness of breath. It got worse and worse, and harder to breathe. I looked at the roadside call box. I wanted to call an ambulance, but the call boxes were NOT accessible to those of us who cannot hear. As I neared home, I could hardly breathe. I rolled down the car window to catch my breath. Immediately upon entering the house, I dialed 911. They were supposed to be TDD accessible. No answer. I dialed again, tapping and tapping on the keyboard to inform them that a deaf caller was trying to get through on their TDD. No answer! I hung up and went across the lawn to my neighbor's house. Thank God, she was home. I told her to call 911. An ambulance arrived within minutes. I was whisked off to the nearest hospital where it was confirmed that I had a mild heart attack. Upon my release from the hospital, I was furious about not having access to 911. I filed a complaint with the Department of Justice. It so happened that another Deaf woman in Southern California had a similar experience, and had also filed a complaint. Janet Reno, who was the Attorney General at that time, heard about the complaints in California about failed accessibility. I was contacted by the DOJ to work with them on implementing a better system. I referred the DOJ to NorCal. As a result, California got an accessible 911 program for deaf/Deaf users. Today, while most Deaf people have moved away from TDD's and now use videophones, Deaf callers needing emergency 911 services do have telephone access nationwide, for both TDD's and videophones, 24 hours a day.

During my tenure at NorCal, I was on the Sacramento Disability Advisory Commission (DAC) for four years. All of the people on the DAC have some kind of disability, and represent the needs of people with disabilities. In 2005, 20 years after I left NorCal, the DAC needed a Deaf person to join and represent the needs of the local Deaf population. I was hesitant to take on this responsibility because by this time, I had retired from the State and was teaching ASL part-time at a private school. My son urged me to join, arguing that I would still make a good representative for the needs of our Deaf community. Upon reading the results of a survey of the Sacramento area, I was quite surprised to learn that the Deaf and hard of hearing had the least accessibility of all disabled groups. I knew that I had a new task ahead of me!

The mental health programs in Sacramento received some funding, but there were no services for the Deaf/hard of hearing. My first goal with the DAC was to get a qualified counselor, knowledgeable of the language and culture of the Deaf, available to us. We got one. We also worked together toward getting basic ASL training for the Emergency Preparedness Committee so they can communicate with deaf/Deaf persons in the event of an emergency. NorCal Services for the Deaf and Hard of Hearing later got involved into this too. They helped push for accessibility. Later the DAC got captioning for all local county Board meetings shown on the local cable access channels. The things we accomplished together toward better accessibility and understanding of deafness/Deafness are too long to list. It was a joy to work with all the wonderful members on the DAC.

Between times I pursued my first love, teaching ASL and educating people about deafness. Through the years I have continued speaking engagements, educational workshops, mentoring, and fundraisers. It has always been my hope that people who hear will understand our culture and our continuous struggle with *audism*[2]. I have met with hundreds of Deaf people. This enabled me to share their feelings, lives, and viewpoints, and write about how we as a population, and as individuals, broke the sound barrier. As I said earlier, I wanted to write this book for many years, but was not ready. As shown by you reading this, I'm finally ready.

---

[2] The term "Audism," and its definition, appears several times in the book

Acknowledgement

I would like to thank the many people who made this book possible. First and foremost, I thank all of my Deaf friends and acquaintances who willingly shared their life stories with me. This enabled me to write about them in my book, giving my readers insight into the personal lives of the Deaf. I thank the few hearing parents of deaf children, who accepted their child's deafness and found great joy in having a deaf child. All the stories in this book are of real people and true incidents in their lives (however, all names have been changed to protect their identities).

My friend Judy (Tingley) Viera, who helped me get the first ASL class set up at Sacramento City College in Sacramento, California back in 1976. That class led to all the other local colleges in the area offering ASL classes, and Sacramento having the most amount of ASL classes offered in any city in the country. This could not have been done this without your help and support, Judy. Thank you!

Mr. Willis Mann, who was not only my boss at NorCal Center on Deafness, but also my mentor and friend, who gave me lots of guidance toward developing skills and knowledge. Thank you!

My former student Peggy Selover, who helped write AB 51, to add ASL sign language to our State of California high school curriculum, but also to Mel Carter, Larry Fleischer, Tom Humphries, Ella Lentz, Ken Mikos, Susan Rutherford, and Cheri Smith for working together with Peggy to help get AB 51 passed. This bill later influenced other states to follow their leadership, and have ASL added to their college curriculums as well. Today ASL is the fourth most studied language in the nation. We cannot thank all of you enough.

My longtime friend and "advisor," Joanne Jauregui, who never stopped pushing me to get this book written. You always believed in me. I love you.

Rebecca Kindblade, for her help and advice. Rebecca, being a child of Deaf adults (CODA) clarified what should be added, as well as advising changes. Thank you. You are wonderful!

I thank those who took time to look at some of the drafts, and advised me on their thoughts and suggestions: Kathleen Robinson, Caleb Lopez, and Ellen Thielman. Then again, my friends Willis Mann and his wife Jackie, who took the time to review the chapters and gave me helpful comments and advice.

My daughter in-law Stephanie Hester-Diamond who would not let me get discouraged and give up. Your love and support meant so much. What would I do without your help and guidance? You never failed to give me positive feedback and encouragement, Thank you.

Finally, and most importantly, my patient and wonderful son, Brian Diamond, who helped so much with the editing, research, and advising me on making additions and expanding topics. This book could not be published without your many recommendations. I love you. Thank you for making my dream come true.

Part I

MY INTRODUCTION TO THE SOUND BARRIER

"Blindness separates people from things; deafness separates people from people."

Helen Keller

Chapter 1

MY EARLY YEARS

As a young child, I remember lying in bed and listening to the sounds of crickets outside my bedroom window. When I heard the crickets, I always thought of the movie "Pinocchio" and of the cricket in the movie. You may remember his name. It was Jiminy. I thought he was so cute and wished that I had a friend like him. Childlike imaginings would race through my mind and I'd wonder if Jiminy had come to play with the crickets outside my window. I always believed he had. Then I'd smile to myself at the chirping and drift off to sleep.

My early childhood was normal and happy. We lived on a one-hundred-acre apple ranch in northern California. "We" were my four older brothers and my father and mother. Our nearest neighbor was almost a mile away. Because of this, my brothers and I spent a lot of time on our property playing together. We always had something to do. We'd often go swimming or fishing for trout in the creek up the road. We would swing out on our makeshift rope over the creek and drop in. Sometimes we'd swim in our swimming hole, a secluded pond. We climbed the apple trees, sat and sang songs, or jokingly made fun of each other. A little redwood grove was also part of our property. My brothers built a tree house there and used it for their hiding place. Of course, I was never allowed in the tree house. It was strictly "boy stuff."

We had to help out on the ranch by picking apples every morning before we were allowed to play. Our father had a loud, booming voice that one could hear above all the other sounds. So in the morning when I'd hear the family stirring, I'd usually jump out of bed before my father had time to call to one of my brothers to fetch me. I didn't like to hear his loud voice.

On Sundays, my mother and father took us to church where we would all sing glorious Christian hymns. On special occasions like Easter, I was asked to sing solo in front of the congregation. My voice was soft and sweet—pleasing to those who listened. My parents beamed with pride as their "little green-eyed blonde angel," all dressed up in her Sunday best, sang in church for all to hear. After the service there were always people around me exchanging pleasantries, but I'd rather go to the car in the hope we would leave because I was very shy. Talking to people was not my favorite pastime.

What I really loved was getting back to the ranch, changing clothes, and with our Australian shepherd, Blackie, in tow, heading for the apple orchard. Hidden among the hundreds of apple trees was a big, old cherry tree, which I loved to climb. Here I could be alone with Blackie, who always ran around the tree yapping and barking, angry with me because I could climb and he had to stay down. After a while, he would realize that I was not coming down, so he'd curl up on the ground and fall asleep in the warm sunlight.

I'd be alone in my own world, up in the cherry tree with only the chirping of distant birds and the soft thud of an occasional apple falling to the ground. I'd indulge in cherries for hours while I sang songs to myself. In my childhood fantasizing, I was a great opera star and I'd let my low voice become high-pitched and sophisticated. On occasion, I'd hit a really high note and Blackie would wake up and look at me with his ears perked. Finding my singing nothing to get excited about, he'd go back to his nap.

My wonderful childhood years, much like those portrayed in Norman Rockwell paintings, came to an end one chilly fall evening. I remember rising that day to the sound of voices as usual and taking the two-mile walk to school with my brothers ahead of me, laughing and talking as I tagged along behind them. They were talking about the movies we had seen the month before and how maybe that night our father might agree to let us go to the new movie that had come to town. It was a big thing to us back then. Our father would sometimes agree to let us go if we had helped with the apples all month.

I remember being a little worried that maybe I would not be able to go because I did not feel so well that morning. I dallied along behind my brothers thinking of one movie we had recently seen. It was "Bambi." I had become upset when the bad hunter shot and killed Bambi's mother, and poor little Bambi had cried out in a helpless and abandoned voice for her. It had made me cry and cling to my mother's arm in the darkened theater.

By the time we got to school, I felt even worse. My head hurt and my body ached all over. It was such a weird feeling, like nothing I had ever felt before. I told my teacher, and she sent me to the school nurse who found that I was running a high fever and said I should go home. Every step of the walk home was an effort—it felt like someone had put concrete in my shoes. My legs seemed so heavy and the road home so long. By the time I rounded the bend that led to our house, I was exhausted. I was grateful to find my mother alone in the kitchen, baking apple pies. But, even the smell of freshly baked pies did not make me feel better.

Seeing me and hearing how sick I said I felt, my mother stopped baking and wrapped me in a clean blanket, just off the clothesline. Then she carried me over to the rocking chair, cradled me in her arms and rocked me back and forth. As she rocked, she began singing to me in her gentle, soothing voice. Tucked into the warm, clean smelling blanket and lulled by Mother's voice, I soon dozed off.

I woke up a bit later to find that my mother had tucked me in bed. I could hear voices in the other room. She and my father were discussing my illness and whether or not my mother should go ahead and take my brothers to the movies. But I was so tired and sleepy that the conversation did not really get my attention. Then I heard our car pull away in the distance and my father was standing over me, soothing my hot brow and telling me to go to sleep.

I remember telling him I was very thirsty. He brought me a glass of water and held it for me to drink. Then he tucked me in and spoke softly, telling me again to go to sleep. He said for me to rest and I'd feel better in the morning. It was one of the few times I had ever heard my father speak softly to me. It was comforting. Grateful for his love and caring, I closed my eyes. I could hear the radio playing in another room. Frank Sinatra was singing "The House I Live In." ... *The house I live in, a plot of earth, a street. The grocer and the butcher and the people that I meet. The children in the playground, the faces that I see ... all races and religions, that's America to me ...*" Sinatra's soft, baritone voice was soothing to me. My head hurt and I felt very warm from fever. I drifted off.

I do not know how long I slept, but when I awoke, I lay for a long time straining my ears for some sounds of life. There was none. I thought I was dreaming. I fell back to sleep. When I woke up again, my father was bending over, feeling my forehead and talking to me. I could see his mouth moving, but I could not hear him.

"What did you say, Daddy?" I asked, wondering why I couldn't hear him and then wondering why I couldn't even hear my own voice. He spoke to me again and, puzzled by my expression, moved closer to me and spoke again. Finally I said, "Daddy, I can't hear you!"

Suddenly my mother and brothers appeared. There were quick movements and confusion. One of my brothers ran through the apple orchard to get Dr. Karloff, who lived down the road. The doctor took one look at me, bundled me up and drove me to the hospital. From the corner of my eye, I could see, but not hear, my mother becoming hysterical. At the hospital, I was diagnosed with spinal meningitis. I was seven, and would never hear again.

I had to remain in the hospital for a long time. I was very unhappy, of course, because I felt so isolated and alone. The world suddenly seemed so quiet. I couldn't hear the radio any more. I was confused when the nurses tried to talk to me. Most of the time I just stared up at the ceiling wondering why I could not hear. I missed my brothers and wondered why my mother never came to see me. It was only my father who visited every day. When my father would come in, I'd cry and beg him to take me home. He tried to explain why I had to stay, but I didn't understand. When tears welled up in his eyes, I only cried more.

Finally, the big day came; my mother and father were taking me home. I was so excited that I jumped out of bed to show them how well I could walk. But my walk was not straight, nor would it ever be (many people who become deaf as a result of spinal meningitis, or other illnesses, lose some of their sense of balance). My mother had brought my pretty pink dress and she made a fuss over my hair, brushing it again and again while we waited for the doctor to come in and talk to them. Then, at last, I was sitting between them for the ride home. I didn't know why my parents appeared to whisper to each other so much, but I was so excited and anxious to get home to my brothers that I didn't pay too much attention.

Sadly, my homecoming was not what I had expected it would be. My brothers were outside waiting for me when the car drove into our driveway. Each of them hugged me, one at a time. But the hugs were quiet and withdrawn. Years later, I came to understand that my mother and father were not the only ones emotionally shattered by my deafness. My brothers were deeply affected too.

Once the initial shock subsided, life returned to normal, more or less. Things were as much the same as they could be, yet they were different too. We still sat around the big, round dining room table at dinnertime. The difference was that now I always sat between my father and mother, instead of next to my brothers. Instead of being able to quiet down on my own when I slurped my soup or hit plates with my utensils, I had to be made aware of these noises and taught how to be careful and control the noises.

When there was conversation at the table, either my father or mother would nudge me to let me know that someone was talking. I would peer up from my food and watch the person who was talking, then try to eat some more, only to be nudged again to let me know someone was talking. I tried to watch the speaker and eat my food, all the while trying to learn how to lip-read from the side. I was made a part of the conversation, even though I hardly understood a sentence that was being said. I still talked verbally to my family, only now they had to tell me when I talked too loud or too low. I learned to control my voice and raise it when necessary. My father still spanked me when I got all "high and mighty," but now it was not as hard.

My parents made it clear from the beginning that I was still their daughter and that my deafness need not isolate me from the family. We still gathered around the radio to hear the news after dinner (one of my brothers would be assigned by our father and mother to tell me part of what was being said so that I would know what was happening in the world).

My brothers and I still played together, climbed trees together and did other kid stuff the same as before. The difference now was that my brothers went out of their way to make other kids understand that "my sister can't hear" and that I needed to be tapped on the shoulder when spoken to.

Everyone accepted it ... or else! My brothers stood up for me, so I was safe and protected. I was just one of the guys, only I had a little "blemish."

I remember asking my mother when I would hear again and if I would ever get well. She tried to explain to me, moving her mouth slowly, but since I was not yet able to lip-read well enough to understand what she was saying, I believed what I wanted to believe.

As I adjusted to my silent world, the time came for me to be fitted with a hearing aid in the hope that I would be turned back into a "normal child." The problem was, I had lost almost all of my hearing and would never benefit from the use of a hearing aid. I remember returning to public school and having to sit in the front of the classroom so I could watch the teacher's lips. I hated it when the teacher would say something to me, because I could neither hear nor lip-read well. I'd stutter and look around helplessly. The other kids would start laughing. I'd put my head down and let the tears roll down my cheeks, glad my back was turned to my classmates.

This went on for a long time. One day, in a desperate attempt to hear again, I turned up the hearing aid full-blast. It made a loud, whistling noise which, of course, I could not hear. Not knowing how to explain the situation to me, Mrs. Underhill, my teacher, ran to find one of my brothers in the next classroom. My brother took me into the hall and told me about the whistling (by then I could lip-read my brothers better than anyone). When I understood what had happened, I peered into the classroom and saw all the kids talking about me and laughing while Mrs. Underhill tried to quiet everyone down. I couldn't take it anymore and, for the first time since I had lost my hearing, I became angry and rebellious. I snatched the hearing aid out of my ear and, with the cord swaying at my side, I ran toward home.

Along the way, I became exhausted and out of breath from running. I sat by the road on a little hill and cupped my face in my hands with my eyes downcast, unaware that a car was approaching. The driver saw me, stopped the car and got out. When I looked up, I was surprised to see my father standing over me. He could see that I had been crying for a long time, so he put his arms around me and held me close to him. I told him that I couldn't hear with the hearing aid and sobbed all my frustrations to him. I believe it was right then, for the first time, that he accepted the fact that I was totally deaf, because a short time later I was sent away to a residential school for the deaf.

"I take the position that you do not teach Deaf culture, you absorb it."

I. King Jordan
Former Deaf Gallaudet University President

Chapter 2

MY NEW WORLD

The drive to Berkeley was long and tiresome. My mother looked sad all during our trip. I asked her if she was crying and she hugged me, smiled, and said, "No." I sensed a big change was coming in my life, but I could not understand what it was at such an early age.

We finally arrived at the California School for the Deaf. It had high towering old brick buildings built in the late 1800's. It looked like scenery out of "Oliver Twist." The driveway looped up to the building and back to the street. In the middle of the driveway was a circle of grass, with an American flag on a flagpole standing in the center. Next to it stood a towering bronze statue of an Indian fending off an attacking bear. I did not know it at the time, but a noted Deaf sculptor named Douglas Tilden created the statue (Tilden also has his work displayed in San Francisco's Golden Gate Park as well as Candlestick Park- the old San Francisco 49ers and San Francisco Giants stadium). I wasn't sure if I should be scared or excited. One thing was sure: the architecture and environment looked just like the Oliver Twist movie and I could feel the isolation and the loneliness that Oliver experienced.

A very wide concrete stairway led up to the main office from the driveway. Inside I was introduced to the school superintendent named Dr. Elwood Stevenson. He was a tall slender man with soft graying hair and frameless spectacles. He had a gentle smile. He shook hands with me and told me to sit down, motioning with his hand so I would understand. His kind and gentle manner made me feel comfortable as I sat between my father and mother. While they talked, I amused myself by looking around the room at all the old books in the large floor-to-ceiling glass bookcase. I studied the old portraits of bearded and mustached men on the walls. I was not aware at the time that they were pictures of past superintendents of the school. They were all people who were not Deaf (that still rings true today). Then I studied the things on Dr. Stevenson's desk, entertaining myself with my little girl imagination. When it was time to leave, Dr. Stevenson shook my hand and told me he would see me again soon (at least, I think that is what he said). I held on to both my father and mother's hands as I walked between them down the long, wide concrete stairs to the car for the long drive home.

A month later, we drove back again and this time I was to stay at the school. The housemother, Mrs. Luken, greeted us. She was a tall slender woman with her graying hair and a nose that reminded me of a bird's beak. She seemed kind enough, but I did not feel any sense of motherliness in her, like I had sensed the fatherliness in Dr. Stevenson. After hugging my father and mother, Mrs. Luken took my hand and led me to the dormitory. I glanced back at my parents. My mother was crying so I began crying too and did not want to go with Mrs. Luken. I sensed she figured I was going to be a problem child, because she gripped my hand even tighter and pulled me along with her. I wanted to pull away and run back to my mother, but as a child, I never rebelled against anyone (especially my father). So I reluctantly went along with Mrs. Luken. My heart was filled with a terrible sadness.

I did not realize it at the time, but this would be my transition. This would be my home for the next 8 years. This was a residential school for deaf children from age six and up. Here I would learn to lip-read and sign. I would be exposed to role models who couldn't hear—just like me. The other kids would become my brothers and sisters because we all lived together in the dormitory, ate, played, and attended classes together.

Once settled in the dormitory, I noticed all the other girls my age talking with their hands. Since I did not know sign language, I shied away from them and stayed by myself. I missed my mother and wanted to go home and play with my brothers, at least they knew how to communicate with me in the way hearing people do. I cried a lot and the other girls did not know what to do with me, so they left me alone. I was the weird new kid on the block. I did not like the school at all. I could not hear, and I could not talk to anyone because the other kids used a language I did not understand, nor had seen before.

One day after school, as I climbed the concrete stairway, I stopped in a little benched alcove half way up the stairs. I sat and watched the other girls pass by me with their hands flying. Everyone just ignored me. I figured that deafness meant loneliness and isolation. I was confused and unsure what they were saying. I was thinking how much I wanted to go home and hated this cold, confusing place. Then a scrawny blonde girl with little round glasses came and sat beside me. She was obviously the popular kid because all the kids followed her around and sat near her wherever she sat. She smiled and began signing and teaching me the alphabet in sign language. She told me her name was Joyce and showed me her name sign (many Deaf who use sign language have a name sign given to them by other Deaf people, especially if they attended schools for the deaf. The name sign fits the person's personality, habits, or interests). When I understood that she had given me a name sign, I became very excited. Soon a lot of other girls gathered around me. Then, another girl who seemed like a leader of the pack, came up and told the other girls to move over because she wanted to sit by me! She joined Joyce in teaching me how to sign. I learned her name was Bernice and that she and Joyce were the leaders of the group. At first, Bernice and Joyce taught me the hand alphabet, then some words. But after a while, they got bold and told me a vulgar sign. All the girls giggled and covered their mouths with their hands. So I knew it was something forbidden and I laughed too, even though I was not quite sure what the sign meant.

From that day forward, Joyce and Bernice took me under their wings and taught me many signs. I followed them around all the time like a little puppy dog. Soon, I could sign quite well and I was a lot happier, because now I was "one of the girls." Most of the girls became my friends for life because we developed a bond. Residential schools are unlike public schools where kids go home every day at 3:00 PM. Students in residential schools stay there all the time. Back then, we only went home at Christmas, Easter, and during the summer. Today, kids at residential schools go home every weekend.

As I became more fluent in sign language, I understood more about the world of the deaf. I learned via signed information that a Deaf man created the bear/Indian sculpture in front of the entrance to the school. I also learned about the other kids' deafness. Some were born deaf, some were hard of hearing, and some became deaf later, just like me. Nobody seemed to care if you were totally deaf, hard of hearing, or became deaf later. We were all just a group of kids that could not hear, that's all. I saw how the parents seemed to accept their kid's deafness and let them grow up with their peers rather attend a public school. The parents appeared to understand that their deaf children would have a happier life in a school for the deaf. I sometimes saw those parents who lived nearby come to the school to volunteer, bring their kids cookies, or attend teacher's conferences. I was surprised to find out that there was a college for the Deaf in Washington, D.C. which was attended by Deaf students from all over the world. I found out that Dr. Stevenson was also the son of Deaf parents. He had become like a surrogate father to me over time.

One year after I had entered the school, my mother died of cancer. My father, overcome with grief, turned to alcohol. I spent my summers in a foster home. However, Dr. Stevenson called me from class into his office frequently, just to ask me how I was doing. He would always smile and welcome me. He made me feel special and important. He and his wife Edith often invited me to their home, to have dinner with them. Their home was at the edge of the campus. It was a beautiful old two-story house built in the 1870's. It had a third story that I always wanted to climb the stairs to see, but Edith told me it was merely a window in an attic. Over time, the more I discovered about other Deaf people who had been successful in life, the better I felt about myself. Many of my teachers were themselves Deaf and were role models for me. "If they could do it," I thought, "so can I." It also helped that my parents and brothers had accepted my deafness. They never tried to change me, criticize me, or overprotect me. I had a good start there.

The school always had plenty of activities planned for us after classes. After learning sign language and making friends, I became involved in sports. Sports were something I looked forward to when classes were over. We had swimming, track, volleyball, and baseball. I found I was good at all these. That was probably because I grew up with four brothers. I always played a lot of sports with my brothers, which made me tougher and stronger than most girls. Pretty soon, I started getting ribbons in a variety of competitive sports. It was fun. My girlfriends and I would laugh, play, and then run back to the dormitory to change. Then we would go to eat in the big dining room with long tables all the way down the building: little kids at the first table, bigger kids at the second table, and so on until the oldest kids were at the end of the last table. Each table held four boys and four girls. At the heads of each table were older girls and boys who helped monitor us. Every meal started out with a prayer in sign language by the boy's head counselor Mr. Birck. Meal times were fun because we could talk to the boys. Sometimes one kid at the table did not like this or that and we would exchange food, give each other our Jell-O or cake, or whatever one of us liked in particular. It so happened that one of the head table guys was an older student who I met again in later years and married.

One of my favorite teachers was a Deaf man named Mr. McArtor. He was extremely handsome and looked like Douglas Fairbanks from the movies I saw as a young child. I thought he looked a lot like my own handsome father. Mr. McArtor gave us fascinating and interesting stories every Sunday night. We would all gather in the auditorium to listen to him via his signing stories. I also thought how wonderfully he would "paint" signs in the air with his beautiful sign language while telling us adventuresome stories. Every Sunday night he would tell us a different story. Then, close to the very end, and about to reach the height of story, he would suddenly stop and look at his watch and say, "Oh, time is up. I will finish next week!" He knew very well that we wanted to hear the end of the story. He always did that to tease us. Of course, the reaction was always the same. We would all stomp our feet loudly on the wooden floor and wave our hands in protest! (Deaf people do not holler verbally like those who hear. We stomp the wooden floor and wave our hands in the air when we are "hollering") These Sunday nights were so much fun. He inspired me to sign, mime, and be expressive like him. But then, all Deaf people are by nature, expressive.

Another teacher that influenced me was again a Deaf man, Leo Jacobs. He was both my Math and English teacher. I discovered early in my life at that school that I was poor in Math, but good in English. I laugh now remembering how he once told me back then "You will never make it in Math, Lois, but you could probably make it as a writer someday!" He loved my essays and always encouraged me to write more. He often kept me after class to go over what I wrote about and discussed my writing style, English etc. Mr. Jacobs later wrote, <u>A Deaf Adult Speaks Out</u> (Gallaudet College Press 1974).

During my residence at the California School for the Deaf, I attended speech and lip-reading classes and was taught how to control my voice and pronounce new words. One summer when I was in my foster home, my classmate Paula lived not too far from me. I was allowed to go on the bus to visit her home. Arriving at her house, I met her mother. I shook her hand and verbally said, "Hi. I am glad to meet you." She looked at me with a shocked face and said, "You can talk?" I said that I had gone to the school's speech classes. I did not understand why she was so upset, until years later. What transpired was that she called the school and was very angry that Paula could not talk like I could. The school tried to explain that Paula could not learn to speak like me because Paula was born deaf and that I had become deaf later in life. Her mother would not accept that. She felt Paula would be more normal if she could speak. She insisted that Paula take the speech classes and learn to talk! What happened after this was Paula did attend the speech therapy classes. Over and over, she was taught to say some words, and then taught a sentence. For example: "The moon is full." Poor Paula struggled over and over: "Theeee moooonith fooool." Following that, Paula came home and spoke the sentence to her mother. Her mother was absolutely thrilled. She called all her relatives and told them that Paula could now speak. Relatives swarmed her home and Paula was put on display. Speaking for them, Paula said, "Theeee moooonith fooool." Everyone clapped. Her mother was so proud to now have a speaking child. After a while, her mother told Paula to say something else. Paula said she only knew ONE sentence. Her mother was devastated. Her child was not made "normal" after all.

As I grew older and began to fill out, I started taking an interest in boys. I noticed the older girls had boyfriends and would bring their shirts to the dorm, wash and iron them and then give them back to their boyfriends. I wanted to be grown up like that too. I picked one of the nerd kids I sat with at the dining table to be my boyfriend. I told him I would wash and iron his clothes for him. He got excited and brought me a bag of clothes. When I got to the dorm, I looked in the bag only to find he gave me a bag of underwear to wash! I was so mad and hid the bag so my girlfriends would not see it and laugh at me. The next day I returned the bag with a note that said, "I changed my mind. I do not want to be your girlfriend. We are broke up."

Like public schools, we had annual prom dances. Public schools had proms called Junior and Senior proms. Instead, we had what we called the Fellow's Athlete proms and Girl's Athlete proms. It was basically the same thing with just another name. We got all dressed up like girls do. The boys came to the dormitories with corsages and escorted us to the dining room for a banquet. A lot of the teachers, both hearing and Deaf, attended the banquet and watched proudly as each of their students came through the door all dolled up. Following the banquet, we went to the auditorium. During the summer at my foster home, I had learned to Jitterbug (the "in" dance during the 1950's) so I was on the floor for every dance and wore my date out! Back then, we did the "Bunny Hop" where we all lined up in a chain dance together. We got to do that the last hour before the closing of the dance. When we all went back to the dorm with our dates, there were a lot of chaperones there to make sure we didn't pull any monkey business. We deliberately spread out from each other in the dark, knowing the counselors couldn't see every one of us, so that some of us could sneak kisses from our boyfriends and the counselors/chaperones wouldn't catch us! Of course, when we all got back to the dorm, we gathered and yakked about all the fun we had and what happened. We were just like a bunch of giggly girls who could hear. We also had football games, both at the school and away. We had cheerleaders too. I was one of them and that was so much fun. We also had a girl selected for Homecoming Queen. I was selected once. It was not because I was the prettiest girl. It was only because my boyfriend at the time was the school's football star.

My life at the residential school gave me the opportunity to be just like kids who could hear. If I had gone to a public school, or "mainstream school" as they are called today, I know I never would have had all these wonderful role models, been involved in competitive sports, been a cheerleader, or a Homecoming Queen. Rather, I would probably be isolated and quiet. I might be the same fun loving person that I am, but I doubt that I would become the strong leader that I have become without all those role models. Also, all my school activity participation made me feel equal and confident and led me to stand up for my rights like I do now.

I am grateful to my family and the teachers who helped me develop my character and strength. Because of them, I grew up to be a happy, strong, and positive person who felt it was okay to be deaf.

Graduating from the school was another emotional experience. As hard as starting out there had been for me, leaving was even harder. It meant saying goodbye to my "brothers and sisters" that I had grown up with for nine months out of each year. It was like leaving home for the first time, scared of being out on your own and knowing that you can never come home again.

After graduation, many of us went to Gallaudet University in Washington, D.C. This is another beautiful campus with rolling lawns, trees and older brick buildings built back in the middle and late 1800's. A five-foot-high brick wall surrounds the campus, and there was only one entrance. I felt that going there was like entering a "Deaf Disneyland." Not because there were rides and cartoon characters, but because **everyone** there spoke in sign language just like at the California School for the Deaf. It was wonderful to see and meet Deaf people from all over the United States, and some from abroad, signing to one another. American Sign Language (ASL) is not universal, and other countries have their own sign language. It was fascinating to see foreign Deaf people signing their own sign language while learning American Sign Language—just like hearing foreigners do when they learn English. Gallaudet was both a fascinating and happy world. Everyone talks to everyone there and almost everyone knew everyone else. It was very unlike the outside world, where there was so little communication with those who could hear. Inside the walls of Gallaudet University, strangers talked to strangers, made friends with each other and went off campus together for football games, movies, shopping and dates (yes, we were free to hold hands and kiss there).

Gallaudet University was another place that was hard to leave. Going out into the world of those who hear, and joining the work force was difficult for me. Other than those who had been taught sign language, very few people who could hear signed back then. It is far different today where there are hundreds of sign language classes, thousands of interpreters and where many people who can hear sign or have had some exposure to Deaf people. When I was learning the ropes of the outside world, I was dating a hearing man who did not sign. We got along fine via lip-reading, as long as it was just he and I because I had been taught to be an excellent lip-reader. However, when we went to parties with other people who could hear, it was difficult for me. If we went to a party with a lot of other people, who hear and did not sign, someone would tell a story or joke and I did not understand. My date would say, "I'll tell you in a minute." Then after everyone finished laughing, my date would turn to me and tell the story again. But now everyone watched me to see my reaction. Even if I felt it was not funny, I would laugh at the end of the story, just to be accepted. In the world of those who hear, I could not be myself. With people at school, we all signed and nobody cared if you laughed or not; they were too busy enjoying themselves! Nobody was any different from each other at California School for the Deaf or at Gallaudet University. We were **kin**. In the world of those who hear, things were different.

The years after I left Gallaudet are when I discovered my identity more fully. **I am Deaf.** I accepted that I am not a person who can hear, and I need not try to be. There was no need to try to impress someone to accept me. I accepted myself and was proud of who I am. I am not the only Deaf person who feels this way. Most all of us Deaf feel the same. We take pride in our Deafness and ourselves and go about our lives.

Part II

SOME HISTORY AND CULTURE BEHIND THE SOUND BARRIER

Note from Lois: *We are now moving away from my own personal experience of becoming deaf and being introduced to the sound barrier, and into Part II, where I look at some history and culture of many Deaf and hard of hearing people who have lived behind the sound barrier.*

In Chapter 3, I present the controversy and history in communication methods of those who do not hear. As you read through Chapter 3, remember that I was born hearing and became deaf at age seven. I was fitted with hearing aids, my family helped me learn to lip-read, and I was sent back to public school. I depended on the teacher's facial expressions and body movements while trying to lip-read. I hardly understood a word the teacher said. When I was sent to the California School for the Deaf, I learned sign language. For the first time since becoming deaf, I could understand everything that was said to me—not just some things. I no longer had to walk across the room to look at the lips of the person speaking, hoping to catch parts of what was being said. With signing, I could understand 100 percent, and I was so happy to be "hearing" again. Being among others who also signed, my world was so different—and better! I now understood the difference between struggling in the hearing world of spoken language versus smooth communication where I would never experience that kind of struggle anymore. I believe this is partly why I have taught sign language over 35 years in a variety of settings to thousands of people who hear. I know their signing would be a blessing to other Deaf people. I write from my own life experiences, so my opinions are on one side of the debate presented in Chapter 3.

Chapter 4 shows how being deaf can also become more than just an inability to hear.

"In the deaf community, there are different types of people who have different philosophies. Some believe that they should only sign. Some believe they should only speak. Some say you should use cued speech. Some say you should use cochlear implants. Some say you shouldn't sign. Some say you should sign."

Marlee Matlin

Chapter 3

MEET THE HATFIELDS AND MCCOYS

Back when I was in my 20s, after I left Gallaudet, I thought that all deaf people signed. I was shocked when I learned that some deaf people never used sign language. Some deaf people learned to lip-read and speak, with the belief they could function better in the world of people who speak and hear. I was surprised to learn that there are two distinct paths in life that a person with hearing loss might follow: learn to sign, or try to speak and lip-read. Deaf people who use sign language are known as "signers." On the other hand, deaf people who do not use sign language as their primary means of communication, but instead choose speech/lip-reading, are known as "oralists." If you ask a Deaf person who uses sign language why signing is better than oralism, you'll get a long lecture about the wonders of signing, and the evils of oralism. Ask a deaf person who rejects the use of sign language why he or she prefers speech/lip-reading and you will get an equally long lecture about how oralism is the best way to go, and why signing is bad. A lowercase or a capital "d" when describing deaf/Deaf indicates the difference between oralists and signers. I will further explain this in the next chapter.

I had no idea that going to a residential school for the deaf and then to Gallaudet was not just part of my education, it also became part of my identity in life. When writing this chapter, I felt I needed to get an oralist's point of view, so I would better understand, and not be closed-minded about deafness, and think that signing was the only way we should all live.

That's when I found out that oralists and signers have *very* different ideas about deafness. Why did some deaf people not sign? Why such different beliefs of which type of communication we should use? How did this all come about? There is a long history of signing versus oralism that goes back to the late 1800s. I have often referred to the argument between the deaf/Deaf as the "Hatfields and McCoys." Like that legendary dispute between the two mountain clans, both sides INSIST that they are right and fight over the issue. So who is right? As with the mountain clans, neither is right (although I began Part II giving my own personal experience). Often, it is the method our parents choose for us on the advice of some well-meaning medical doctors. An overview of the history of educating the deaf will help my readers to better understand the deaf/Deaf Hatfields and McCoys analogy.

The dispute began in the 1870s, with two well-known educators of the deaf, Edward Miner Gallaudet and Alexander Graham Bell. Both of them had deaf mothers and both of them worked in deaf education; but they had two very different beliefs on how to best educate the deaf. Bell believed that deafness was something that needed to be eliminated, and one way to help accomplish this was for the deaf to learn to lip-read and speak, so they could function in the hearing society. Gallaudet believed deafness did not limit the intelligence of people that could not hear, even though the deaf used a different method of communication.

To truly know why they had different beliefs, you have look at Gallaudet's and Bell's fathers. Around 1815, Thomas Hopkins Gallaudet, Edward' father, became interested in deafness and deaf education when he saw a group of children playing and noticed that one little girl (his neighbor's daughter) was deaf, and how she kept to herself and didn't play with the other kids. She was a nine-year-old named Alice Cogswell who must have stolen Gallaudet's heart, because he became determined to educate Alice and other deaf children. When Gallaudet checked into deaf education programs, he found that only private tutoring was available, it was oralist, and it was expensive. Gallaudet wanted to find a cheaper and maybe better way to educate the deaf, so he traveled to England, Germany, and to France. While in France, he met Laurent Clerc, an educator of the deaf, who himself was deaf. Clerc was using sign language to teach his deaf students. Gallaudet asked Clerc to come over to America with him.

In 1817, Gallaudet and Clerc opened the very first school for the deaf, the American School for the Deaf (ASD), in Hartford, Connecticut. Would you believe that ASD is still operating to this day?! Thomas Hopkins Gallaudet later married a deaf woman, one of the graduates of the school, and they had eight children together. Two of those children, Edward and Thomas Jr., went on to work in deaf education. Edward Miner Gallaudet began working at ASD at age 18, and later established the first college for the deaf in the United States. He opened Gallaudet College (now Gallaudet University) in Washington, D.C. in 1864.

Alexander Melville Bell, the father of Alexander Graham Bell, worked with the deaf and those who had difficulty speaking. He taught speech by using symbols that showed the position of throat, tongue, and lips in making sounds. Alexander Graham Bell taught his father's method and vocal techniques. Like Gallaudet, Bell also traveled to other countries to educate the deaf.

Alexander Graham Bell was invited to teach this method at ASD. There was openness and acceptance to oralism by Gallaudet and others that supported sign language. However, Bell insisted that oralism was the ONLY way for the deaf to be educated. Bell believed that signing separated the deaf from those who could hear, and that deaf people should be taught to listen and talk. So this was the starting point of the "Hatfields and McCoys."

Today, it is a very common belief in the Deaf community, and I am one of the believers, that the oral method is successful mostly for those who are hard of hearing, or those who had hearing and learned the sounds of speech before becoming deaf—like I did. The difference between people who had hearing for some amount of time before becoming deaf, or are hard of hearing, compared to a person who was born profoundly deaf and has never heard the sounds of speech, is a very, very important difference. Those who are born profoundly deaf and never heard the sounds of speech, struggle to succeed in oralism. In these situations, the deaf person is labeled an "oral failure." Because I was born hearing and had speech before I became deaf, and went to school with deaf children who were born deaf and never heard the sounds of speech, I dislike any "oral failure" label. It is very unfair.

Alexander Graham Bell also married one of his deaf students. Her father helped finance Bell's experiments in the electrical transmission of speech with the hope they might help the deaf to hear. Instead, Bell's experiments resulted in the invention of the telephone. Ironically, this "accident" benefited those who hear instead of those who were deaf! After Bell invented the telephone and established the Bell Telephone Company, he now had both the fame and the money to spread the oral method.

The major event in deaf history that separated supporters of oralism and supporters of sign language was the International Conference on Education of the Deaf in Milan, Italy in 1880. Representatives at this conference voted to stop the use of sign language in schools in favor of the oral method. Students of Deaf History argue that the outcome of the Milan Conference was prearranged by having almost all oralism supporters—both as speakers, and in the audience. There were a total of 12 speakers, nine in favor of oralism, three in favor of sign language. Edward Gallaudet and his brother Thomas Gallaudet Jr. were two of those three speakers who supported sign language. Deaf children who were taught the oral method, and were successful cases, were "paraded" in front of the conference members to show how wonderful oralism was. Edward Gallaudet argued that these children were hand-selected as extreme examples, and because these children had not become deaf until after the age of seven, they had already acquired some speech and had a small amount of hearing. Therefore, these children would not truly represent the outcome for most deaf children learning the oral method. Also, at this conference on the education of the deaf, 162 of the representatives were hearing. Only **two** were deaf! After the voting at the Milan Conference, public schools in Europe and America banned sign language, and only taught oralism to their deaf students.

Gallaudet disagreed with the vote, and when he came back to America, he insisted that sign language continue to be used at his college. Many of the deaf residential schools in America also continued to teach signing. Keeping with the Hatfield and McCoys analogy, this is where the battle lines were drawn. Supporters of Bell and supporters of Gallaudet were on separate sides from that point forward.

There is more to me and other Deaf people/signers not supporting Bell than just disagreeing with his philosophy on how to best educate the deaf. Alexander Graham Bell was one of the first supporters of eugenics. Bell believed that deaf people should not be allowed to marry one another so they would not have more deaf children (I married a Deaf man, and our children are hearing). Bell opposed a Deaf culture and Deaf social clubs. His goal to completely eliminate sign language in America often came at the price of cruelty to many deaf children. It is well-known among us in the Deaf community that some schools that taught "oralism only" in the late 1800s and early 1900s, tied the hands of deaf children behind their backs, and forced those deaf children to communicate by trying to speak. Knowing this history, and because eugenics is strongly related with Adolph Hitler and WWII, most people in the Deaf community would never support oralism and those who support Alexander Graham Bell—back then, or today.

Although I went to a deaf residential school where sign language was the way of communication, the oral method was the most common system for educating the deaf for the first half of the 1900s. A shift started to happen in the 1960s when research done on ASL by William Stokoe at Gallaudet University concluded that ASL is a true language, complete with its own word order and structure, like spoken languages have. Stokoe's research began to change the perception of sign language. Then, the passage of the Vocational Rehabilitation Act in 1965 made it possible for sign language interpreters to be paid for interpreting. These two things helped sign language to gain more support.

"In This Sign," a book written by Joanne Greenberg in 1970 about Deaf parents who always seemed to misunderstand many things until their hearing child explained it to them in sign language, brought more attention to sign language. Around this time, some of my Deaf friends and I talked about how the school systems were questioning the methods of deaf/Deaf education. I'm not sure if it was Joanne Greenberg's book, or William Stokoe's research, but there was discussion with educators and psychologists about why America had many confused and apparently uneducated deaf/Deaf people. The oralism supporters and sign language supporters lined up against each other and debated on what should be done in schools to educate the deaf.

When the Rehabilitation Act of 1973 was passed, it required federal government agencies to be accessible to the deaf and hard of hearing, and provide sign language interpreters. As a result, sign language use and sign language interpreters started to appear in schools and federal government agencies in the late 1970s.

I remember some "types" of sign language being experimented with in the 1970s, which led to me teaching ASL classes at Sacramento City College in 1976. In the Preface of this book, I wrote about how I became a teacher of ASL classes at Sacramento City College after I first saw (and was confused by) SEE[1] and SEE[2]. The intention of SEE[1] and SEE[2] was for deaf children to learn English. Seeing Essential English (SEE[1]) is a separate sign for each syllable of a word. An example of this would be the word "highway." The syllable "high" would be one sign, with another sign for the syllable "way." The meaning and context of the word is not what is important—the only intent is to teach the *sound* of the English word. Even though I had hearing until I was seven, and could speak and lip-read fairly well, this was so confusing to me!

Signing Exact English (SEE[2]) was signing words exactly as they are spoken or written. Although many words in the English language have many different meanings for the same exact word—depending on its context— with SEE[2], the words are signed based on a two-out-of-three rule: spelling, sound, and meaning. If a word meets two out of the three criteria, that word is signed, regardless of its correct use. Think about the word "beat." Someone can beat an egg, beat a sport team, or physically assault another person. With ASL, there are three different signs for those three different ways the word "beat" is used. Yet, in SEE[2], an alternate word or sign is *not* used to clarify the meaning. As you might imagine, this caused quite a bit of confusion and misunderstandings in educating those who cannot hear. What I have always taught, and every ASL instructor teaches, is that ASL is *not* spoken English on the hands. Today, SEE[1] and SEE[2] are far outdated. However, you may meet Deaf people today who learned to sign this way during that time period. When I met Deaf people that grew up using either SEE[1] or SEE[2] we would often struggle to understand some of each other's signs.

Something that also helped bring ASL more into the mainstream was the Broadway play "Children of a Lesser God." That play showed the isolation of the deaf, and how we were angry at those who can hear because hearing people made all the decisions for us and allowed us no "voice" in anything. You may already know that "Children of a Lesser God" was made into a movie, and in 1987, Marlee Matlin won the Academy Award for her role in the movie. I was so thrilled that she won. It showed the world that deafness does not limit us. I also loved that "Children of a Lesser God" presented a lot of truth about being deaf, and showed some of my frustrations as a Deaf person. I also remember that after the movie and Marlee Matlin winning the Academy Award, ASL classes in the colleges really began to grow.

The use of sign language has come a long way. As I write this, sign language is the third most used language in America, and the fourth most studied language. However, the oral method has its supporters, and the "Hatfield and McCoy" debate continues today.

For this chapter, I did some interviews with oralists and signers, as I wanted to get a good understanding of both views. These interviews truly revealed to me the difference between the thoughts of those who use the "oral method" and those who use the "manual method," which I knew nothing about when I was young.

Interview 1

I met Mark through mutual friends and told him I was writing this book. I explained that I wanted to get his viewpoint of why he chose the oral method over signing. He agreed to have dinner with me and to share his feelings about his life as a deaf person.

Mark became deaf as an infant due to an undiagnosed illness. He grew up in a wealthy family, was raised by the oral method, and learned to speak to the best of his ability. His father owned an import/export business, and Mark was given a job in the company that required little communication with the public. He married a hearing woman, and they had two daughters.

As we dined, we communicated through speech and lip-reading. He told me about his life and how happy he is in his world. He said that if he used "the sign" he would not be as successful. "Signing," Mark said, "separates the deaf from the hearing world and limits signers to the Deaf culture; it also limits them in learning and understanding about the real world out there." He went on to say that signing makes the Deaf uneducated.

Then, noticing my reaction, he added with a laugh "of course you are an exception ... " Being the good sport that I always try to be, I smiled back, and asked if he had ever tried to learn sign language so that he might understand the difference. Mark replied that his family would never allow him to sign and "fling his hands around like some crazy animal." I wanted to respond to this comment, but instead continued to listen to his story. After all, I wanted to get his opinion, and since he was nice enough to agree to dinner, I didn't want to offend him. I was reasonable enough to accept the fact that, although we both did not have the ability to hear, we were two different people with two different viewpoints. It was similar to what would occur if an immigrant from a traditional family and an immigrant who had become "Americanized" sat across the table from each other and discussed their views. They share common ground, yet a different perspective.

Mark went on to describe how he had traveled all over the world and visited many places. Our conversation was difficult for me to understand at times, especially when he told me the names of cities and countries he had visited. I wished he could finger spell those names so I could at least be clear about the places he mentioned. But, since he was enjoying himself so much, I chose not to interrupt him to ask that he repeat the names. When we finished our dinner and were parting, I thanked him for sharing his life story with me. He then took my hand, kissed it, and looking up at my face so I could read his lips said, "This is how they do it in France," and laughed.

<u>Interview 2</u>

Marilyn, who became deaf at age 2, was also brought up with the oral method. I met her at one of the coffee socials where Deaf people and sign language students often meet for the students to practice their ASL skills. She told me her life was fine and happy, but by chance saw an interpreter at a hospital who was interpreting for a Deaf woman and the doctors via signing, and she was fascinated. Out of curiosity, she decided to enroll in a sign language class.

After some time learning sign language, Marilyn said she realized how much information she had missed, and that her life was not as "fine and happy" as she had thought it was. She told me, "For the first time, after learning to sign, I could walk into a room full of Deaf people and 'hear' the conversations as I gazed from person to person." Then she giggled embarrassedly and looked down at the floor signing "Now I can 'hear' all the dirty jokes too." She said that prior to learning sign language, and using the oral method, it was always a "one to one" conversation, where she only knew what was being said by one person at a time.

Interview 3

Carol, who was born hard of hearing and later became completely deaf, grew up attending the John Tracy Clinic until she was seven years old. Carol then attended a different school that used sign language. At first, she was not comfortable signing, and liked the oral method better. Over time, she became skilled in signing, and realized how much more comfortable she was being able to sign and fit in with others who signed. Carol said she could understand so much more now. This made her happier because she did not have to experience the constant struggle of lip-reading all the time. Having learned signing, she felt she understood things 100 percent now, instead of partly understanding when she used lip-reading only. However, she said she was glad she could both sign and speak/lip-read because it helped her to communicate with the outside world.

Interview 4

Pauline, who was born deaf, told me she is very happy with signing. She had wonderful friendships with other Deaf people and hearing people who signed. She said she could understand everything, and grew up comfortable in her signing environment.

She said she could not imagine being forced to lip-read and speak all her life and struggle to understand some communications. ASL gives her full access to her signing world. She insisted strongly that ASL is the best, most wonderful and beautiful language—as well as the easiest way to communicated for all those like her who were born deaf.

After these interviews, I started to think about how most oralists and signers do not have the opportunity to experience and compare both worlds, or perhaps refuse to do so, because they are often set in the ways that they were taught to believe. As deaf children, we become caught up in the path set up for us by our parents, our teachers, or some well-meaning, but unaware family doctors. Still, it was interesting to me to find when I interviewed people who were raised by the oral method and then later learned sign language, that they did not return to the oralism-only method. I also interviewed John F. Egbert, founder the Deaf Bilingual Coalition (DBC). The goal of the DBC was to inform parents of deaf children the importance of deaf children learning both ASL and English. The DBC encouraged both ASL and English to improve the cognitive development of deaf children and wanted to inform parents of deaf children, and the public, of the resources and support available, and the successes of Deaf people.

Egbert was born deaf, and went to a school that taught the oralism-only method. He pointed out that he was one of the success stories of oralism, and learned to speak better than most of the other kids at his school. Egbert told me that after the third grade, he was placed in a public school with hearing children. At this public school, he struggled to read the lips of the teachers, and gained most of his learning by reading the textbooks.

After high school, Egbert attended Gallaudet University, where he was first introduced to sign language. Like many others that I have met or interviewed, it was at this point when Egbert found a whole new perspective. He told me, "With sign language, communication becomes a 'two way street,' in that I communicate with you and you communicate with me using a shared language. However, with the oral method, it is a 'one way street,' where it is just me trying to read your lips and me being the only one who struggles to understand what is being said. Also, if there is more than one person in the room who is speaking, I feel lost and isolated."

Egbert explained to me that, after many years, he realized that the oralism-only method focused just on the ability to speak and read lips—but paid no attention to cognitive skill development. This occurred to him especially when playing with his deaf grandchildren who communicate through sign language. Egbert saw that his grandchildren could recognize sarcasm and humor. When comparing his childhood being raised with the oralism-only method, Egbert realized that he didn't really have an understanding of language and meaning like his grandchildren did when he was their age. Egbert told me that while he may have been able to speak, his cognitive development was lower. As a grandparent, Egbert now understood that *education* should be the primary goal for deaf children, not their ability to speak.

The goal of the DBC was to expose parents of deaf children and others in the hearing community to the benefits of bilingual education. Egbert and Deaf members of DBC felt that parents and followers of the oralism-only method are not given all the information they need to make an informed decision on how to best educate deaf children. This is partly because leaders of AGB are all hearing people[3]. Egbert pointed out the National Organization for Women (NOW) is run by women. African-Americans run the NAACP. The Gay and Lesbian Alliance against Defamation (GLAAD) is run by gays and lesbians. However, AGB is run by *hearing* people.

Back in June of 2008, the DBC organized a peaceful protest at the AGB convention in Milwaukee. Jumping at the chance to be heard, many Deaf people from all over America came to the AGB convention to protest the "speech only" method. The protests got newspaper and TV coverage, and for the first time, Deaf leaders and members of the Deaf community were allowed to have their feelings publicly known on the debate of oralism versus sign language.

In 2015, the battle of the Hatfields and McCoys took a very, very surprising turn here in Sacramento. After fighting each other for about 135 years, leaders of the oralism community and leaders of the sign language community worked together to pass a legislative bill! For maybe

---

[3] In 2015, there was one deaf leader at AGB

the first time ever, both communities found they could agree on one area of deafness: that deaf and hard of hearing children are language delayed by age five when they arrive in kindergarten classes. Leaders of the California Association of the Deaf, NorCal Services for Deaf and Hard of Hearing, and the California Coalition of Options Schools joined together to pass SB210, which requires the California Department of Education to test and set standards for deaf and hard of hearing students in language development and literacy. Until 2015, getting along and agreeing has never happened! It was such a shock to me! Yes, I do support sign language first. But, it is my hope as a Deaf person who has benefited from both American Sign Language and English that the "Hatfields and McCoys" can somehow work together across the country and continue what has started here in California.

All of us at one time or another have wrongfully assumed things. In this chapter, you read how I incorrectly assumed that all deaf people used sign language. In the next chapter, you will see that deafness is much more than being a "signer" or an "oralist," and many wrongfully assume that deaf people are all the same.

"He who knows one 'deaf person,' knows none."

Based on a quote by Max Muller

Chapter 4

DEAFNESS: HEARING LOSS OR A CULTURE?

Many times in my life when I told people who hear that I am Deaf, the first thing that person does is start talking louder; or they try to get their mouths closer to my ears, as if volume alone could overcome deafness. This has often irritated me, and made me angry for years. However, over time I have mellowed, realizing that people who hear do not undertand the difference between being hard of hearing and being deaf. This same experience has been relayed to me by Deaf friends as we share anecdotes about our deafness. We all laugh about it, but it is not really funny. People who hear do not intentionally offend us, they just lack knowledge about deafness. We feel that it may be because many people who can hear think that all deaf persons are the same. The truth is, all deaf persons are NOT the same. There are varying degrees of hearing loss and it generally falls into one of three basic groups:

1. Hearing loss that can be helped with hearing aids.
2. Significant hearing loss that would be helped very little with hearing aids.
3. Totally deaf.

The extent of hearing loss may determine how individuals identify themselves and with whom they socialize. For this reason, there is a clear distinction between "deaf" and "Deaf"; the lower case "d" or capital "D" has very specific meaning. In essence:

deaf
This group defines their deafness by a measurement of hearing loss—such as decibel per ear. Generally, these are people who grew up hearing and experienced hearing loss later in life. Although they may have significant hearing loss, they still identify themselves as "hearing" and continue to socialize with, and follow the values of, those who hear.

Deaf
These people, not necessarily born deaf, embrace Deafness as their lifestyle. They identify with the values, history, norms, and traditions of the Deaf. Sign language is cherished and storytelling in ASL is highly respected. Deaf events, Deaf socials, life in residential schools, and Gallaudet University is the common thread.

Along the varying degrees of hearing loss are smaller groups of deafness/Deafness. It is important to know that these smaller groups have less to do with the actual decibel loss of hearing and more to do with how one identifies themselves. A closer look shows the different problems and frustrations within each group.

Hard of hearing (HH):
Those who are hard of hearing do have some residual hearing and can benefit from the use of a hearing aid or cochlear implant (a surgical procedure in which a device that stimulates the cochlea is placed in the inner ear to help restore some hearing).

HH people suffer different kinds of frustrations than those who are totally deaf.

The major issue for a HH person is trying to decide if they fit in the "hearing world" or the "deaf world." Some of the HH deny their physical hearing loss and continue in the hearing world, even with their difficulties. Others acknowledge their hearing loss and they choose (or their family chooses for them) to be fitted with a hearing aid and to live and function in the hearing world the best they can, even if they can only hear minimal noises with a hearing aid. Those who acknowledge their physical hearing loss and find ways to adapt, remain part of the hearing community, and are just that: part of the hearing community. They are unaware of, or are resistant to, the Deaf community.

There are those who are considered hard of hearing, but do not have enough hearing to operate within the hearing community, and then, step into the "Deaf world." There are also those who are hard of hearing, who accept their hearing loss and choose to become part of the Deaf world, and use whatever residual hearing they have to their advantage. HH people often can speak for themselves without the use of an interpreter. Some read lips, or try to fill in the gaps by relying on whatever residual hearing they have left. Hearing people who meet a HH person who operates within the Deaf community may mistakenly assume that **all** deaf people can hear to some extent, or that **all** deaf people can communicate like those who are HH. This is not true.

In some cases, the HH have difficulty deciding where they fit best, so they go through life with a dual personality—being a hearing person by day and a Deaf person by night (I believe this is sometimes done to please their hearing families who do not want to accept their hearing loss). Many HH people actually never become part of either the hearing or Deaf worlds—they sometimes "fall between the cracks." He/she is not hearing, yet, not Deaf. This is parallel to an interracial child; which culture does he/she choose to belong to? Sometimes, he/she is not totally accepted by either. Sometimes, they drift through life never knowing where they belong, and never sure of their identity.

The late-deafened:

These are individuals who have been stricken deaf after hearing their whole lives. The impact of their sudden hearing loss can be (and usually is) catastrophic; the later the onset of hearing loss, the more devastating. To be able to hear one day and learn the next that you will never hear again is one of the greatest tragedies one can face in life. Unlike those of us who lost our hearing in early childhood or who are HH and choose to accept themselves as Deaf, these people do not readily accept the Deaf world. It was not until a few years ago that support groups for the late-deafened were established. Before then, many late-deafened people suffered from depression, isolation, and even committed suicide, leaving family members devastated and many lives forever changed.

The Association of Late-Deafened Adults (ALDA) is a national organization that provides help and counseling for those who suffered a late-in-life hearing loss. In California, there is another wonderful organization formally known as Self-Help for the Hard of Hearing (SHHH). It is now known as the Hearing Loss Association of America (HLAA), which assists those who must deal with hearing loss. Many of the people who work in these organizations endured late-in-life hearing loss themselves. Enough good things cannot be said about such organizations, and some of the finest and nicest people you could ever meet work with them.

Cochlear-implanted children:

Around the year 2000, a somewhat "new generation" of deafness came into society: children receiving cochlear implants at an early age. Cochlear implants are an extremely controversial and widely divisive issue. Parents who hear, Deaf parents, audiologists, medical doctors, members of the Deaf community, and educators have varying and strong opinions about cochlear implants—the benefits, consequences, and effectiveness. The success and results of cochlear implants differ greatly, and several factors determine the outcome. Sometimes hearing is improved substantially, while other times hearing is improved minimally, or not at all. Some hear sounds better, but not well enough to speak on the phone or understand the lyrics of songs on the radio. Some deaf/Deaf adults also receive cochlear implants. These results are varied too. The controversy is mostly over the implanting of children, not adults.

There is concern for the psychological effects that may go with a cochlear implant at a young age, such as the difference in physical appearance and being made fun of by other children for having electrodes in their heads. This can be quite damaging to a child's self-esteem. There is also a concern about negative psychological effects of cochlear implants for children, faced later in their adult years. It is debated which category these children will fall into later in their lives—the hearing world, the Deaf world, or someone with a confused identity. Some people believe that children with cochlear implants will grow up knowing their parents loved them and did what they felt was best, while others believe that the children may feel that their parents could not accept them for the way they are.

Deaf:

I belong to this group. We are just that—Deaf. We do not hear, never will, and most of us have accepted this as part of our lives. There is no such thing as "stone deaf," unless a person has no eardrums. This is extremely rare. Most deaf people have at least some residual hearing. Some Deaf people "hear" loud noise. When we feel vibrations and people that hear notice, they tend to think we are able to hear.

Because those who sign do not communicate in the language of the hearing—the spoken word—we are sometimes looked upon as "outcasts of society." This is something that has been imposed upon us due to our hearing loss. We have been segregated, though not by choice.

Many of us break through our barriers, become educated, hold down jobs, work alongside people who hear, do business with hearing people, and function well in the hearing world. How we adjust is often a matter of personal choice. Most of us have a clear sense of who we are and we accept ourselves. We do not usually make a big issue about not being able to hear, unless it pertains to some kind of discriminatory behavior toward us. We do not normally view our handicap as a disability in the same sense that hearing people view disabilities. We view it more as an inconvenience, and we live with it (Because of the legislative and technical advances in today's world, many of us no longer feel we are handicapped or disabled, but are a cultural and lingusitic minority. This is one of the reasons why I named this book "Breaking the Sound Barrier.")

So as you can see, not everyone with hearing loss is the same. A *culture* is generally defined as a set of people who follow a set of norms, values, behaviors, and shares the same history. When we group "deaf" and "Deaf," there is most definitely a Deaf culture. The bigger picture is how the amount of hearing loss can determine the path of a person's life. There are also other factors that can determine the path of a person's life that has hearing loss, such as their age when they lose their hearing, where they live at the time they lose their hearing, and the influence of their parents. Hearing loss can then become a struggle to hear like those with normal hearing, or it can become a lifestyle and an identity.

Deaf culture usually stems from attending residential schools and being with our own "kin"; that is, those who speak our language—mostly

American Sign Language. That's how I felt in my residential school. My classmates were my brothers, my sisters, my kin. Residential schools top the list for developing a spirit of togetherness, along with Gallaudet University (or colleges with deaf programs). The Deaf we meet and grow up with are considered our "families," and friendships are often formed for life. We form our own Deaf clubs, organizations, and social events. We support the use of sign language as the best way to communicate, learn, and express ourselves. In Deaf culture, signing is considered beautiful and artistic.

Being Deaf is a way of life for many individuals who do not hear. We take pride in being Deaf, readily admit we are Deaf, and let everyone know we cannot hear. We could not care less about how we appear to others. Have you seen Deaf people on a bus or in a restaurant chatting away with their hands, never caring who is watching or what anyone thinks? They accept themselves for what they are and wear it like a badge of honor. Those of us who are Deaf, delight in having Deaf children to carry on our heritage and our culture—while many of those who hear consider it a "tragedy" to have a deaf child. Deaf people have cliques and classes just like hearing people do. Some of us are educated, and some of us never learn to read beyond the fourth grade level—just like those who hear. Some of us are fortunate to obtain prestigious jobs, but some of us are deprived of secure or gainful employment—just like those who hear.

Those of us who are a part of the Deaf culture are a close-knit clan. Our world is a small one where many of us are known to each other. This is due in part because we attend the same residential schools, and those who continue their education are likely to attend Gallaudet University, National Technical Institute for the Deaf, or California State University Northridge. Furthermore, we are a small group in a much larger society, from which we are in many ways still somewhat isolated. When I was young, and for most of my life, we communicated and kept in touch through newsletters and magazines for the Deaf. Now, texting devices, e-mail, and videophones have extended Deaf culture. Since we attend the same events and belong to the same organizations for the Deaf, we tend to talk about mutual Deaf friends. We go to the weddings of our Deaf friends, attend the Bar Mitzvahs, christenings, and graduations of our Deaf friends' children. We cry together at the passing of a beloved teacher or Deaf friend, laugh and hug when meeting "long lost" friends. We also talk endlessly! Why not?

Those who hear can listen to the radio and enjoy music or talk shows. Deaf people live in a quiet and sometimes lonely world. Meeting a Deaf friend or an acquaintance and being able to communicate and have shared experiences and a shared culture with them is a very big thing to us. Like those in any other culture, we Deaf people sometimes argue over political issues. However, there are strong bonds and often a lot of love among us. Many people who hear never experience a kinship equal to this in their lives.

People who hear consider it impolite to point, but Deaf people point to each other as a means of clarifying to whom we are referring. We also wave our hands and stomp on wooden floors to get another Deaf person's attention. Hugging and touching is very much the norm. This is all part Deaf culture. People who hear tend to shake hands when they meet, but people within the Deaf Culture always hug. People who hear are often astonished to see how affectionate the Deaf are to each other.

As I mentioned earlier, some people who have hearing loss are not totally deaf, but choose the Deaf culture nevertheless. Sometimes we are born into this culture and sometimes we find it during the course of our lives. People in the Deaf culture draw comfort and strength from sharing stories of the Deaf experience. Sometimes we talk of our frustrations within the world of people who can hear. We struggle with those who do not sign or even try to communicate with us. We talk about our experiences living in their world and among those who stereotype us and think all deaf people are alike. We also talk about our frustrations with those who do not understand us, or how difficult it is to sometimes get promoted in our jobs. We also share information about new and beneficial services for the Deaf. We update one another on mutual Deaf friends—who got married, had a new baby, or became a grandparent. And, of course, we share gossip!

Most of us do not necessarily dislike people who can hear. But, we are more inclined to friendships with hearing people who can sign or have Deaf relatives. That is to say, with those who hear who have some understanding and/or are involved in our community—like sign language students or interpreters.

You may wonder who is within the Deaf culture. The Deaf and HH who go to a residential school usually automatically become part of the Deaf culture. Otherwise, it just happens to those of us who choose sign language over oralism. Being born to Deaf parents gives one this privilege at birth. Deaf people who are born within the Deaf culture are often referred to as "grassroots Deaf." This is because they have been within the Deaf culture most or all of their lives; sometimes from generation to generation, since some deafness is hereditary. Within the Deaf culture, it is considered somewhat prestigious and awesome to have other Deaf relatives. Deaf families sometimes boast with pride about their Deaf offspring. Their family tales are often fascinating and, as you might guess, sometimes exaggerated to get attention and be admired.

Groundbreaking Deaf people are heroes and celebrities in Deaf culture. Some of the pioneers and greats in Deaf history are Laurent Clerc, Dummy Hoy, George Veditz, Bernard Bragg, Linda Bove, Ella Mae Lentz, Carol Padden, Tom Humphries, Marlee Matlin, and I. King Jordan, to name a few. There are also people that were not deaf, but are well-known and highly respected in Deaf history. Among them: Thomas Gallaudet, Edward Gallaudet, William Stokoe, and Lou Fant (a child of deaf adults –CODA).

Today's Deaf Generation

I must acknowledge that I am from an older generation of Deaf people. Most of the groundbreaking Deaf heroes and celebrities I just named are from "my time." Several new generations of Deaf people have come forward. Beginning in the 1970s, and really taking off in the late 1980s, deaf children were taken out of residential schools and placed in public schools with hearing children. These deaf kids were given sign language interpreters who sat with them all day during their classes. These deaf kids are now adults who have grown up around hearing people and without the "culture of Deafness" that the residential schools gave to prior generations. Some may say this is good, while others would argue that our culture is dying. Technology, social media, reality television shows, and the benefits of the Americans with Disabilities Act (ADA) have brought today's deaf kids and young Deaf adults so much more into the mainstream with those who hear. While this is quite wonderful, and life is always about progress, there is a part of us older Deaf who do not want to lose our Deaf culture. Just like immigrants whose children have taken in American culture, there is a bit of sadness that comes with change. There are still residential schools, Deaf social events, and associations for the Deaf, but I have witnessed many changes, and new generations of Deaf are here.

Part III

LIFE BEHIND THE SOUND BARRIER

Note from Lois: *As my readers now have an understanding of some history and culture of deaf/Deaf people, we move into Part III, where I give you an idea of what life is/was like living as a person who does not hear.*

What you will read here in Part III is where some of the ideas for this book first got started. As I wrote in the Preface of the book, throughout my life people have asked me questions about my deafness and about deaf/Deaf people.

In Chapter 5, I answer some of the most common questions asked of me and my Deaf friends.

In Chapter 6, I share some stories of my life and other's lives as Deaf people.

"Just a thought … it is interesting to see that DEAF people can function in the hearing world very well while hearing people cannot function in the DEAF world."

Gil Eastman, Gallaudet Theater Art Professor

Chapter 5

LIVING WITHOUT SOUND

Is it hard being Deaf? How does it feel? How can you drive a car if you cannot hear? What happens when the phone rings and you cannot hear it, or when the baby cries? Is it true that the Deaf people distrust those who hear? These are among the questions often asked of me through the years. When talking with my Deaf friends, they told me that they also have been asked questions by hearing people who want to know how do we live and function without sound, and this is part of the reason why I wrote this book.

My living in this world of silence has been basically a blessing to me in several ways. I believe a big reason for the great friendships and relationships I have had throughout my life is because I am Deaf. I have taught, counseled, mentored, lectured, and advocated for over 35 years. The positive impact that I have had on certain individuals would not have happened if I was not Deaf. The motivation for writing this book is because I have experienced life living in a world of silence. I also believe that I, and most other deaf/Deaf people, are more aware of little things that most people who hear miss out on, like their surroundings and the body language of others. Yet, there are times when I get frustrated by the attitude of some people who hear. Throughout my life, many people would tell me they were "sorry that I was Deaf." I would want to say, "My life is good, and better than yours." However, I was taught by my parents to never be rude or sarcastic to "those well-meaning people."

There are some incidents in my life, and incidents that my Deaf friends have experienced that I can share. While it is sometimes challenging not being able to hear, nearly every deaf/Deaf person has assistive devices[4] in their homes—signal lights that alert us when someone is pressing the doorbell and when the phone rings, or baby criers that attach to the crib and activate a signal light when the baby cries. We use the captioning option on our TV sets and enjoy TV programs. Most Deaf people use videophones and the Video Relay System (VRS) to make phone calls to both hearing persons and Deaf persons.

I have been asked many times by people who hear if deaf people want to hear. In the case of those who experience the trauma of sudden hearing loss or those who are gradually losing their hearing, I would say the answer is most likely "yes." However, for those who have lived without sound all of their lives, or who became deaf at a very early age, and those who grew up in a residential school and learned sign language at a young age, the answer would probably be "NO!" Commonly, we accept our hearing loss much more than those who have recently lost their hearing. Recall the difference between "deaf" and "Deaf." Those of us who are Deaf have adjusted to our hearing loss and have become a part of the Deaf culture. If we could hear, we probably would have different friends—probably who can hear. Deaf people cherish their "Deaf families" who have been with them since childhood. Learning a new culture and becoming part of that new culture would be a huge shock for me, and I think for anyone. Imagine living your whole life as a Latino … and then waking up one morning and you are now Asian! I believe Roslyn Rosen PhD, while at Gallaudet University's Continuing Education Program, expressed it best. During an interview she said: "In our society, everyone agrees whites have it easier than blacks. But do you think a black person would undergo an operation to become white?" Besides, for a person who has lived without sound to wake up one morning to find they could hear alarm clocks, car horns honking, airplanes overhead etc. … that would be frightening! We would have to learn to identify sounds. We would have to learn the sounds of words, spoken language, and how to speak. Hearing again is mostly a beautiful fantasy of those who can hear.

My Deaf friends have said that, like me, they have been asked "Do deaf people hear when they dream?" We are usually amused by this question. The answer is no. When anybody dreams, they are the same person; you

---

[4] Assistive devices and technology is the subject of chapter 8

don't change gender or experience a major age change when you go to sleep—at least I don't think you do! If you hear and speak in real life, you hear and speak in your dreams. On a related note, some people who hear will talk to themselves, do math, go over conversations they will have with someone, and they will actually talk out loud or hear the conversation in their heads. Deaf people do this too! Except when Deaf people talk to themselves, they do it in sign language. On many occasions, I have seen Deaf people trying to figure something out and "think out loud" in sign language.

My children would tell me that they were often asked, "Do deaf people like your mom drive?" A well-known story in the Deaf community for those of my age is that back in the early 1960s, a deaf man accidently ran into, of all people, the car of the governor of California! The governor was very angry and attempted to pass a bill forbidding deaf persons to drive. The California Association of the Deaf (CAD) followed through with a statewide study on deaf drivers. The study found that deaf drivers were in fewer accidents than drivers who can hear! Some may wonder how this could be. Unlike people who can hear, who may have their car stereos blaring or are talking on their cell phones, the deaf are not distracted. They are not fumbling around with their Bluetooth, or trying to adjust their stereo. Deaf people keep their eyes on the road and their mind on their driving (well, most do. With the new mobile videophones, there are definitely a few distracted Deaf drivers out there!). Their world is quiet and focused, unlike the noisy world of those who hear. Deaf people will probably spot an ambulance or police car with a flashing light long before those who hear see it or hear it. They are usually more alert and observant than those who hear. Automobile insurance companies used to charge us double. They assumed we were "at risk" drivers. The results of this survey brought down our rates to the same as those who hear. In light of this study, I say they should charge us less!

Since I began teaching sign language in 1976, and as other ASL classes continued to grow, I have been asked how Deaf people feel about hearing people learning our language. I think most Deaf people would say, "We love it!" Prior to the growth in sign language classes, most Deaf people lived in isolation. Hearing people learning sign language did not erase that, but it was wonderful to find more and more people with whom we could communicate. That has continued to this day. It is nice to be in a store desperately searching for an item and have a sales clerk come up, realize we are Deaf, and sign, "May I help you?" It is comforting to be scribbling out a request for directions at a gas station in a strange city and find that the attendant or one of the customers can sign. When a person is in a foreign country and does not speak the language of that country, it is a wonderful feeling when they meet a person who speaks their language. For a Deaf person meeting a person who speaks their language, that wonderful feeling is even stronger. However, I must say that when the ADA came into effect, and people could make a living as an interpreter, some Deaf people wondered if those who hear took sign language classes did so because of a genuine interest in the Deaf, our language and our culture, or if they saw a gold mine in becoming an interpreter.

I do remember back in the 1980s some Deaf people having trouble maintaining their niceness and patience when they encountered a person who can hear that learned Signing Exact English (SEE²). That is because SEE² was awkward and led to long-winded conversations. Again, SEE² is not ASL. SEE² is an auditory language and ASL is a visual language. ASL fits the way Deaf people think and absorb information. Some Deaf people are not patient, but most Deaf people are always happy to be able to communicate with those who hear.

A common mistake is the belief that every person in the world who lives without sound communicates in a sign language that is universal. In other words, many people believe that sign language is the same in every country around the world. However, that is not true. Every country has their own sign language, just like every country has their own spoken language. The signs are based on the language of that country. In the United States, we have English-based sign language. In America, the word "goodbye" is "adios" in Mexico, and "arrivederci" in Italy. So, Mexico has Mexican Sign Language, Italy has Italian Sign Language, and so on. Yes, there is Gestuno[5]. But, not all deaf people know or use Gestuno, and there can be a language barrier just like for those who hear. However, all signed languages are based on visual communication and gestures; with a little bit of common sense and creativity, Deaf people from other countries can

---

[5] Gestuno is a type of pidgin sign language that uses a lot of gestures and iconic signs. It is also known as International Gesture.

usually manage some communication with each other better than those who rely on oral/audio communication. Barry, a sign language student at one of the community colleges in Sacramento, told me the following story at a Deaf coffee social:

> Barry had taken two classes in ASL and could communicate with Deaf people. One summer, he traveled to Europe. While in Florence, Italy he ran into a Deaf couple, Andre and Lavone. Thinking it would be great to talk with them, Barry began signing in ASL. Andre and Lavone looked at each other quizzically, and then responded with entirely different signs. Barry was flabbergasted, but quickly regained his composure and discovered they were French, and were signing in French Sign Language (langue des signes française, or LSF). Somehow, he was never told that ASL is not universal. Fortunately, Barry's story did not have a sad ending it could have had. The French couple, amazed that someone who could hear would take up sign language, offered to spend their time with him. So, using makeshift signs, they toured Florence together. In a restaurant, Barry rubbed his stomach for "good" when he sampled some Italian food; he patted his face for "pretty" when an attractive young woman passed by. During their day together, Barry taught Andre and Lavone a few words of ASL, and they in turn taught him a few words in LSF. Barry told me that after he got back, he now wanted to learn LSF and go to France.

The thing to learn from Barry's story is that the "A" in ASL stands for "American." When those who can hear travel to a foreign country, they often bring dictionaries that have commonly used words and phrases both in their own language and the foreign language. When Deaf foreigners meet, communication can be easier because Deaf people are natural pantomimes with highly expressive faces. For this reason, it is a great experience to watch the World Games for the Deaf. The athletes from many nations not only enjoy the opportunity to compete in Olympic-style events, but also communicate with each other through different sign languages and miming.

After the wave of political correctness that began in the 1980s, people who hear are unsure, understandably, what to call us or how to identify people who live without sound. One term that I, or any of my Deaf friends, will never call ourselves is "hearing-impaired." That is an expression which came from the politically correct movement, and is used by hearing persons only. The expressions "deaf-mutes" or "deaf and dumb" are very outdated and are offensive to us. It is similar to calling a black person an "Afro-American," or a "Negro." The proper terms for us are simply "deaf" or "hard of hearing." The word DEAF is not a bad word. It's okay to be deaf!

I have been asked if Deaf people distrust those who can hear. To answer this question, let's start by asking if you dislike those of other cultures? Each of you will respond differently, mostly based on your personal experience with the people of that different group or culture. With us Deaf, it is the same thing: an individual response growing out of personal experience with those who hear. Unfortunately, the experience is sometimes negative. This comes mainly from having those who hear take too much control of **our** lives and making too many decisions for us. Often, no consideration is given to **our** opinions or choices. When we Deaf have no say in **our** lives, we are understandably resentful. We want to be able to speak for ourselves and to have what we say heard. Deafness, being the communication barrier that it is, often deprives us of power; being powerless frustrates everyone—hearing or deaf/Deaf. Deaf people usually have no way to release this anger, so it remains within the soul of our being. For some Deaf people, it is worse than for other Deaf people. My ex-husband really struggled with this because he was so intelligent, and was often frustrated because he could not always communicate his thoughts and feelings.

It usually starts with parents. When we are very young, parents tell us what to do, whether we can hear or not. Of course, young children need to be told what to do; they lack the judgment to make good decisions for themselves. However, as children who hear get older, their parents usually allow them to make mistakes and learn from their mistakes. On the other hand, deaf children all too often are kept "little children" by domination and control. Hearing parents feel they must "help" and "protect" their deaf child. Many parents have **fear** for their children. A hearing parents' fear can be oppressive for a deaf child, and most deaf children are not capable of fighting back.

Every minority group in America has stereotypes and oppression that they face. What I just described to you in the last two paragraphs is *audism*. Stereotyping, discrimination, prejudice based on one's inability to hear and taking control of them—intentionally or unintentionally—is called audism. Almost every minority group in America has advocacy or civil rights organizations. We have some too. The oldest and largest is the National Association of the Deaf (NAD), and the newest is the Deafhood Foundation. Like other civil rights and advocacy groups, both the NAD and the Deafhood Foundation seek to educate society about Deafness, Deaf Culture, Deaf History, and above all, to end audism.

Audism can be found throughout America. For instance, how many mainstream schools and school districts have Deaf parents on the PTA or on the Board of Education? Usually none. So who makes the decisions on the best way to educate our Deaf children? Those who can hear, of course. When visiting doctors, many are very busy and don't feel they have the time to consult or communicate with Deaf patients. Many don't want to take the time or expense of having to be bothered to set up sign language interpreters—even if it is the law. Instead, they discuss issues related to our illnesses with family members who can hear. These family members often end up making decisions for us and invading doctor-patient confidentiality. Many Deaf adults feel that in the workplace, most employees who can hear do not ask us for our input as a co-worker. Deaf people who have experienced these things from childhood to adulthood are likely to feel dislike toward the dominant group. Happily, there is often another side to this kind of experience. I met a very interesting student, Cindy, at a Deaf coffee social. I was watching her sign, and she seemed very pleasant, so I introduced myself. We started a great conversation and she told me the following story:

> Cindy had been Deaf since the age of two. As a child, Cindy had decisions made for her by her parents, just like any other young child. Fortunately, her parents later learned sign language and treated Cindy like her other three hearing siblings. By having good communication, they began to let Cindy make decisions as

she grew older. In the beginning, Cindy attended a mainstream school. She was the only Deaf person in the class. But when she was 12, she told her mother she wanted to attend a residential school for the Deaf so she would have more friends like herself. Both of her parents agreed. After graduating from residential school, Cindy landed a job as a data processor. Luckily, her supervisor had a deaf child and could sign. Cindy was promoted over the years. She was provided with an interpreter when she asked for one. She took part in company staff meetings and participated in decision-making. She met a fellow employee who was a sign language student, and they became friends. She also made many friends among co-workers who could not sign, but nevertheless felt comfortable with her.

Cindy's experience is that she was able to be part of both the hearing world and the Deaf world. She likes people who can hear. She was accepted by those who hear. She was happy in their world, participated in it, and was respected in it. After that meeting, we became friends. I still connect with her to this day.

Cindy's experiences are true for some of us who are Deaf. Unfortunately, many of us have lived or still live in a world where everything is decided for us by those who hear. We are resentful of this; we want to be treated with respect as adults, not like unequal children. True, some of us may not be well-educated, but that does not mean we do not think or feel.

The wonderful thing about Cindy's story is that it shows positive change—this story would have never happened 30 years ago. I hope that in the future, many more classes on Deaf culture and history will be offered in schools, and the next generation will continue to better understand those who live without sound. If not, you the reader, must give this book to everyone you know!

Sounds You Never Shared With Me

What are those sounds amid this mystic world I see?
Why can't you share those sounds with me?
Is it so hard, for those of you who can hear,
To share my curious wonder and soothe my fear?

I watched as snowflakes converted the barren hills into a silver crown
The wind blew softly, a snow laden branch came crashing down

Far above, I saw a blue bird fluttering in a tree.
Was I imagining it, when I thought he sang for me?

Tonight a golden moon crept down upon the fallen snow
If coyotes are howling in the distance, I do not know

Crystal chimes tinkle from an open window
beneath the moonbeams light
What echo is heard when they break the silent fields so diamond white?

Is there no sound, but just a beauty that only my silenced world can see?
Or could this be God's way of sharing the
sounds you never shared with me?

Lois Diamond
1974

Chapter 6

MISSING INFORMATION

I was one of the few lucky Deaf people who received a lot of information about the world around me ever since I became deaf. In my youth after becoming deaf, my brothers were all told they had to tell me everything. My father was adamant about that. They were scolded if they did not help me with information that I needed. Looking back, I am so very grateful to this wonderful man who was my father. He truly helped shape my life and made sure I got the information I needed. I am sad that other hearing parents with deaf children did not do what my father did for me. Very few Deaf friends have told me that they got this kind of support and this made me sad. I was always told about sounds around me. Radio, wind, heavy rain, noisy restaurant etc. I was always told the correct way to say something verbally, right way to say a word, songs being played on the radio, and what people around me are talking about. Then in later years, my hearing children told me in sign language a lot of things like latest news, jargons that people who hear used, even taught me song lyrics, funny things people said etc. Unfortunately, I have yet to meet a Deaf person who had this same wonderful experience that helped me develop so well. They never had the advantage that I had. Receiving information is key to developing intelligence and understanding the world. A lack of complete information limits awareness. Deaf persons are born with the same level of intelligence we would have had if we were born with normal hearing. The difference is that people who cannot hear are often deprived of complete information necessary for our development.

We all benefit from environmental sounds; as human beings, it helps us understand more clearly what is taking place in the world around us. When a situation or event is so quiet "you can hear a pin drop," it informs people how quiet or sad an event is, and sometimes, how to act appropriately. When a sign language interpreter explains to a Deaf person how a speaker's voice sounds, such as the speaker "sounds angry," "sounds bored," or "sounds nervous," that gives us important information outside of just the words being spoken. Being made aware of the sound of an annoying car alarm, soft music, or several babies crying at once makes us understand the effect on a presentation or the mood in the room. All of the new technology beginning in the 1990s has made a big impact on our access to information. The Internet, text messaging, e-mail and video phones have made it possible for millions of people who do not hear to stay current on what takes place throughout the world on any given day, at any given moment. Even with all the new technology, I and every other deaf person still miss out on the sounds that are a part of ordinary everyday existence.

To emphasize the effects of missing information, let us consider television. Television provides access to global news, but until the early 1990s, minimal information was available through television to those of us who do not hear. We had no clear idea of what news broadcasts were reporting and could only try to glean what we could from the pictures that accompanied the stories. I've always felt watching TV without captions is like a person who hears watching TV with the sound turned off. You just miss all kinds of information.

Although closed-captioning began about 1980, broadcasters were only captioning a handful of shows until the early 1990s. I can remember when Jay Leno took over the Tonight Show in 1992; it was the first time I ever saw the Tonight Show with captions. For all those years when Johnny Carson was on, I never knew what was said in the show opening. I had no idea that the current events of the day were joked about, or that the president and the government were being made fun of every night. I never knew what the guests said when they were being interviewed. After the Tonight Show became captioned, when musical guests were on the show, I could see what the lyrics were. I was not able to hear the music, but now I knew what they were singing about. The Tonight Show being captioned was extremely welcomed by Deaf/deaf people. We were now able to discuss political jokes and world affairs along with our Deaf issues—something rarely done in the past.

Closed-captioning provided large amounts of missing information for us—information about pop culture, politics, music, and the English language that I believe many people who can hear just take for granted. I urge people who can hear to ask yourself: How many words do hearing people use in their daily vocabulary, but do not know how to spell? They often use these words because they HEARD other people use the words in conversation, on a newscast, in a lecture etc. How many times do people have an opinion on an issue because they HEARD it debated on a talk show? Often, people who hear will voice an opinion as if it their own, simply because they heard other people say it. Deaf people can't hear Rush Limbaugh's radio show (or have the good fortune of not being able to hear it!). Furthermore, many slang words are not understood by us Deaf. What is "cool," "trendy" and in fashion, is often learned through your hearing.

I can't say enough about closed-captioning opening up a whole new world of information for me and other people who do not hear. Research has shown that deaf children not only learn a great deal about sound and receive intellectual stimulation by watching the simple captioning in cartoons and other programs for young children, but they also learn to read better and faster. When we stimulate their understanding about things that they do not hear, they grow up to be more intelligent and aware. Deaf adults too, have expanded their knowledge by seeing captions on TV and becoming connected with sounds and ways of communication. I know that for me, it is both funny and informative to watch a cartoon when one mouse socks another mouse and there is a big "WHACK!" ... "POW!" ... "THUD!" ... on the bottom of the TV screen. I will never forget the first time I saw those words on the screen when closed-captioning first came out. It blew my mind to learn about those sounds. I remember being so fascinated with the caption on TV that I used to get up early so I could watch the cartoons. One morning my son got up and caught me with my cup of coffee watching cartoons. Amazed, he asked me what the heck I was doing up so early to watch cartoons for? I told him I never heard the different sounds cartoons make on TV, so I was "living" in a hearing world now. He thought that was both amazing and funny. Next time he caught me again, he only smiled. Things like this have a big impact for those of us who do not hear. As crazy as it may seem, it was also "educational" seeing shows like "Jerry Springer" and "Maury" with captions. Not that these shows were truly educational, but I was surprised some people actually talked like that and lived like that!

Information for a deaf person can also be gathered from our families. Unfortunately, many of us were born to families who have normal hearing, but do not sign for their deaf child. Current statistics show that only about 12 % of parents with deaf children learn sign language to communicate with their child. The information that would have stimulated their child's understanding and learning process is lost. Sadly, these children grow up deprived of information and of the bonding that comes with fully communicating with their family.

I was fortunate because my family went out of their way to inform me of things and clarify sounds that I no longer remembered or did not understand after losing my hearing. As mentioned earlier, my mother and father made certain that my brothers accepted this responsibility. My hearing children continued this chain of responsibility of sharing information—both sounds and current events. My children were even better because, unlike my brothers, my children sign fluently. They started telling their Deaf father and me things when they were quite young. When they were older and better understood our needs, their desire to share information with us became more intense. They often interrupted our dinner conversation to relay a news bulletin on TV or something funny said on a sitcom. They shared the sounds of things around us, music, jargon and, well, just about everything. Some people were surprised at how much I knew about the ways of the world of those who hear. In truth, I was just like any other Deaf person with average intelligence and education. The difference was that I had the benefit of having my family share so many sounds and general information with me.

I recall many years ago one of my sons, Lance, sitting on the floor by the fire at Christmas time, listening to his little portable radio, playing with his toy soldiers and apparently humming to himself. I watched him from the kitchen, admiring the sweet serenity of his face and expression. It was obvious to me that he was listening to something that brought him joy. Curious, I dropped my chores and went and sat down beside him in front of the fire. I asked him what he was listening to. He told me with the cute, little flying hands of a seven year old that he was listening to his favorite Christmas song. "What is it?" I asked. He replied that he was listening to "Do You Hear What I Hear?" I did not know that song. I had never seen it interpreted, and there was no captioning on TV at the time. "Can you teach me?" I asked. He made a little face and said he would try. He quickly pushed my hand onto the radio and turned up the volume so I could feel the vibrations. He told me which instrument was playing, at the same time miming the instrument. Then he began signing, pausing between the words to again explain the instrument sound or tell me "This is slow, Mom" or "Now there is just a soft echo in the background." As I "listened" intently to his little fingers and facial expressions, I felt goose bumps slowing rising up my arms and neck. I had learned a song that I had never heard before in my life.

After this memorable incident and seeing the great pleasure and happiness he had brought me, Lance made it a point to run up to me whenever one of his favorite songs was played, signing excitedly "Christmas song, Christmas song!" He would take my hand and run to the radio where he would sign for me while I kept my hands on the little black box and "listened." I was to learn several more songs that way over the years from both my son Lance, and my other son, Brian, who also took pride in explaining and signing music for me. Lance is grown now, and has children of his own. But, every Christmas I remember that gentle little boy who warmed my silent world with love and taught me so much. This kind of information is rarely relayed to the average deaf person, who would benefit so greatly from a family sharing.

Being deprived of sound and information affects each of us in different ways and to varying degrees. Many people do not realize there are a lot of deaf persons who enjoy music—whether it is music that is captioned on TV or a DVD, or musical theater with sign language interpreters. Something I emphasize throughout this book is that not all deaf/Deaf persons are the same. Those of us who lost our hearing later in life, or who are hard of hearing, enjoy the privilege of music with closed-captioning. It is not right to stereotype deafness and believe that all people who are deaf/Deaf do not enjoy or understand music. It all depends on the age of the onset of the hearing loss, and sometimes on the person's education and their families. Very few Deaf people enjoy music for the simple reason that they have never been exposed to it as children. The earlier deaf children are exposed to music, theatre and the arts, the more knowledge, appreciation, and understanding they will have when they grow up. Luckily, with the passage of the ADA, deaf people of the last few generations had the advantage of closed-captioning and having skillful sign language interpreters who are involved in musical and performing arts interpreting—which has helped to break the sound barrier.

The majority of us Deaf, especially in early childhood, were deprived of explanations. We were too young to demand to know what was going on. Like all children, we were at the mercy of our environment. Being young and dependent, we could not know the difference between the right way or wrong way of being treated. It was not until we were older and could look back on our childhood and recall how it was, that we realized it could have been much better. I highly encourage every family that hears and has a deaf child to communicate and share as much information with them as possible.

In my many interviews to gather information for this book, I came upon a common scenario for those Deaf whose lives began in isolation:

> Paul, deaf from birth, was born into a family who never communicated with him in any form of sign language other than "homemade gestures." He told me he didn't know what sounds were. His family did not share conversation, laughter, noises, or even jokes. He was puzzled by the very word "sound" because no one had ever attempted to describe to him such common sounds as those of an airplane, car, telephone, or thunderstorms. When I told him that almost everything in the world has a sound associated with it, he replied, "I never knew different things had different sounds to them, I thought everything was just noise."

When he was born deaf, Paul's family assumed he would never amount to anything. What his family did not realize was that it was **them** who were keeping Paul uninformed and unaware. Because he was raised in a closed off environment, Paul and others like him grow up not interested about the world around them. They go through life with no complaints about being deprived of knowledge. They accept the limited scope of their lives as normal for the Deaf.

Strange as it may seem, Deaf persons like Paul often turn out to be happy. They often are not aware of the information they are missing. Those like Paul always received little information and do not crave more; they remain passive. They are often just happy that things are better for them now than when they were children. However, even with access to interpreters at musical performances today, Paul is an example of someone who would not benefit from seeing songs in sign language because he was never exposed to music as a child.

It is much different for those of us who received ample information and communication as children, or for those who lost their hearing later in life. We become very frustrated with the limitations imposed on us by society (Audism). We crave more. We want to expand our intelligence and become better informed. Anger and frustration over being deprived often drives such people to take charge of their lives and become leaders in the Deaf community. They are the ones who fight for better access for us, more sign language interpreters, improved services, and better education for deaf children.

I found out something about sounds, by complete accident, which really floored me. I was in an elevator with my friend who can hear and can sign. We were riding in an elevator when she suddenly began to sing in sign language and dance a little by herself. I looked at her and asked her what the heck she was doing. She said she was singing along to the music in the elevator. "Music in elevators?" I asked. "Yes," she said, "there is music everywhere. It is in the stores, elevators, restaurants, malls, every place." "Are you telling me that people who hear can listen to music everywhere?" I asked her. "Yes" she said. I was shocked! Nobody had ever told me this! What in the world?! When we finished shopping, we went to eat. As I quietly ate, I could not resist the temptation to ask her "Is there music in this restaurant?" "Oh yes, of course" she said. I was shocked again, but felt lucky to learn of this too!

Most of us Deaf find it interesting that people who can hear often do not think to share environmental sounds with us, but seem willing to describe things they see to people who are blind: "We are now entering a narrow room", "the couch is low and covered with brown leather", or "be careful, there are steps in front of you." But, seldom do people who hear tell a deaf person about what is going on in the environment around us such as: "the telephone is ringing," "several fire engines and ambulances are approaching," or "there is music in this elevator." I am sure it is not done deliberately. However, if those who hear shared environmental information with us in the way they do with blind people, many of us deaf/Deaf would, at times, be less confused.

Why is the treatment of deaf/Deaf persons and blind persons so different? I believe this is due in part to the great Helen Keller. Although she became both deaf and blind from spinal meningitis at the age of 19 months, she devoted her life largely to educating us about blindness and improving the lives of the blind. This is ironic since one of her famous quotes is:

> "I am just as deaf as I am blind. The problems of deafness are deeper and more complex, if not more important than those of blindness. Deafness is a much worse misfortune. For me, it means loss of vital stimuli, the sound of voices that bring language, set thoughts astir, and keep us in the intellectual company of man."

I'm sure most Deaf people would love for people who hear to share environmental information. I know that I do. Perhaps telling us that the radio is on and if it music or talk radio; maybe what kind of music is playing. Little things like this help us to understand why everyone is acting the way they are, or what the mood is in the room. It may not seem important, still, we appreciate being told any information that we do not hear. Just a little information here and there is a great act of consideration. Not only does it help us understand the world around us, it also makes us feel good that someone cared enough to take the time to tell us something we otherwise would not know. There are simple things that are really helpful, such as being told "this person has a nice, soft voice" or "all the dogs on the street are barking." We appreciate things like having someone from the office tell us of a flash news report announcing that a bad storm is coming—vital information we may have missed if we weren't recently on the Internet. After all, we have to drive home in the storm too.

Now that my readers understand the importance of information to us Deaf, be aware that most of us would never ask that environmental information be conveyed. We would never choose to burden those who hear, nor feel that it is their responsibility. It is not. We just appreciate this kind and considerate gesture.

Part IV

BREAKING THE SOUND BARRIER: INTERPRETERS, TECHNOLOGY, AND EMPLOYMENT

Note from Lois: *Part IV is where the title of this book comes from. The Americans with Disabilities Act, more than any law in history, not only greatly changed my life, but greatly changed the life of millions of deaf and hard of hearing people across this country—and many of their families. The ADA is the reason all three chapters in Part IV happens—and in this section I write about how after many frustrations and struggles in my life as a Deaf woman, I witnessed how Deaf/HH people as a population, and as individuals, we broke the sound barrier!*

In Chapter 7, I write about the accessibility of professional sign language interpreters beginning in the mid-1990s now meant Deaf/HH joining the mainstream. It brought changes in our daily lives that many may take for granted, such as getting clear, accurate communication with doctors and other medical professionals, or not having to depend on our children to tell us what is being said. I also write about how difficult it is to be a professional sign language interpreter.

Chapter 8 gives my readers some history of life-changing technological devices for the deaf and hard of hearing. For more than half of my life, making a phone call to a family member, leaving a message on a voicemail, enjoying a movie at the theater, or knowing what was being said during emergency warnings on the television, was just not possible.

Chapter 9 discusses the limited employment opportunities I always had, and Deaf/HH of my generation always struggled with. The ADA brought professional sign language interpreters and technology that changed my life in the workplace, and changed employment opportunities for so many Deaf/HH people today.

"Signs are to eyes what words are to ears."

Ken Glickman
Deaf humorist and author

Chapter 7

SIGN LANGUAGE INTERPRETERS

Living my life in a world of those who hear meant often not having clearly conveyed conversations or events. My life was often frustrating, and sometimes hurtful. I know that most of my Deaf friends felt the same. It was difficult not being able to communicate smoothly when I was around people who hear. I was often very quiet because I was not sure of exactly what was being said sometimes. Always trying my best to lip-read, I understood maybe only 30% of what was being spoken. So I remained quiet, rather than make a fool out of myself by saying the wrong thing, or not fully understanding the subject being discussed. This was embarrassing, because once in a while, people wanted me to join in on the conversation and would ask me what I thought. Because I did not feel comfortable joining the conversation, I would just shrug my shoulders and smile, only to embarrass myself even more.

Up until the early 1970s, my Deaf friends and I did not socialize much in the hearing world. Instead, we stayed among ourselves within our own culture, our families, and with the few hearing friends who signed, or took the time to speak slowly and explain things to us. My Deaf friends and I, and many Deaf people across America were not as widely seen by or exposed to the public as we are today. As a result, if a person who can hear met one Deaf person, the impression formed often became a stereotype of *all* Deaf people. Today, the general public better understands us, because over the last 25 years we have joined the mainstream—from the workplace to television and movies. A big reason for this change is the large increase in the number of professional sign language interpreters.

Before the availability of professional sign language interpreters, I, and many other Deaf people, relied on anybody who knew sign language, no matter how little—like family members, friends, neighbors, or members of the church—for most communication outside of our community. For Deaf people who could read and write English, they would use pen and paper. Deaf people with hearing children depended on their children to interpret doctor visits, legal matters, phone calls, and so forth. Hearing children of Deaf parents often suffered emotional strain due to being given too much adult responsibility at a very early age. However, few professional sign language interpreters existed before the mid-1990s, so the children were often given that big responsibility. While I was aware of this with my own children, my husband and I did not have much choice at that time. There are some books written on the subject of what life was like before we had professional interpreters. Some classics are "A Loss for Words" (Lou Ann Walker, 1986), and one I mentioned earlier, "In this Sign" (Joanne Greenberg, 1970). These books show the lives of a Deaf parent long before professional sign language interpreters, captioning, access to telephones, the Internet, and they show the lives of hearing children in the 1930s-1950s whose parents were Deaf. In that era, radio was the main source of information to those who could hear, but was useless to those of us who could not hear. When Americans started getting televisions in the early 1950s, televisions did not come with captions, so Deaf people continued to be deprived of a lot of outside information and entertainment, and we were often confused and frustrated.

In the 1960s, the Civil Rights Movement began changes, including for us Deaf. In 1964, the first organization for professional sign language interpreters, the Registry of Interpreters for the Deaf (RID), was established—in part, with children of Deaf adults. Sign language interpreting as a profession began with several connected events, the setting up of RID in 1964 was the first event. In Chapter 3, I wrote about the Vocational Rehabilitation Act in 1965 when sign language interpreters began being paid for interpreting, and the Rehabilitation Act of 1973 when federal government agencies began providing sign language interpreters. I also discussed how in the late 1970s, deaf children started to be placed in public schools with hearing children and given sign language interpreters who sat with them all day. While many new laws were introduced in the

1960s and 1970s, it was still many, many years until I and most other Deaf people saw professional sign language interpreters in our daily lives. There were still so few available. Very little money could be made as a sign language interpreter. Back then, interpreters were paid very close to the minimum wage. Even after the new laws of the 1960s and 1970s, many of our interpreters continued to be our children or children of our Deaf friends, a person who had a Deaf family member, or fellow church members. Many of those interpreters felt a "duty" to assist the Deaf. Many of them found it rewarding to help and serve. It was looked upon as a personal satisfaction to bring joy and understanding to those who could not hear. If any of us had access to interpreters, we thought they were angels. The following quote by one of the nation's first professional sign language interpreters (he was a child of Deaf parents) really says it all:

> *"The interpreter scene prior to 1964 was so vastly different from that which exists today that it is a strain on the imagination to contemplate it. We did not work as interpreters, but volunteered our services as our schedules permitted. If we received any compensation, it was freely given and happily accepted, but not expected."*
>
> —Lou Fant

In 1990, the Americans with Disabilities Act began the major life-changing period for me and most other Deaf/HH people, and started a big growth in professional sign language interpreting. Part of the ADA required most businesses and public services to provide effective communication for people with hearing, vision, or speech disabilities. This meant more sign language interpreters would now be needed to provide services to private businesses—including medical offices, hospitals, and performing arts centers. It also meant employers who had Deaf/HH employees would now be needing interpreters. Now, there was a lot better pay for interpreters, and a lot more interpreting work available. This change did not happen right after the ADA was signed, but this was the beginning of a life change for me and most other Deaf/HH, and a big part of us breaking the sound barrier.

Back in 1976 when I began teaching ASL classes, I was not teaching *interpreting* classes, I was teaching sign language classes; and before the 1990s, *interpreting* classes were uncommon. To acquire the skills to become a professional interpreter, most people take sign language classes for several years from instructors like me, then go on to a two to four-year interpreter preparation program (IPP). An IPP is much different than what I taught in ASL classes, which was teaching students beginning and intermediate sign language. In IPPs, students learn the entire process of interpreting, which is understanding what is being said in English, and interpreting it into ASL, then understanding the response in ASL and appropriately voicing it into English to the hearing person(s) in the conversation. In IPPs, students learn their role as an interpreter, the grammar in ASL, the different types of interpreting situations, and the laws and rules related to professional interpreting. After the IPP, they usually go through an internship or mentoring period in different settings to gain real world experience. Interpreter trainees also get involved in the Deaf community and participate in events to learn Deaf culture, and learn about the differences in Deaf/HH individual's sign language style. Becoming a professional interpreter will eventually mean needing to become certified; reaching certification is difficult, expensive, and can take many years.

After the ADA was passed, it brought changes in the types of interpreters. It was probably unavoidable that as the field of professional sign language interpreting expanded, more of those who entered it regarded interpreting as a job rather than as a "crusade." Those who previously learned sign language, like most of my students who took my classes at community colleges, did so purely for the joy of learning a new language and culture. Now, many of the students who began studying ASL at the growing number of schools that offered ASL courses, did so because they wanted to earn a living as an interpreter, or because sign language might be an asset in some other profession.

I saw mixed reactions among the Deaf/HH to the growth of the interpreting profession. Some said the changes were wonderful, and were so grateful to have access to communication now, while others said the changes would work against us. One fear was that after many years of working for small wages, interpreters would leave the Deaf community for greener pastures. Another was that the interpreting profession might grow so fast that there would now be many bad interpreters. We did lose some of the "personal touch" which we had become used to. Many of us who once knew our interpreters firsthand, or through mutual friends, now received interpreting services largely from strangers.

In adjusting to the change, we Deaf developed a "code" among ourselves to describe the character and motives of various interpreters. There are three different categories: "Soul," "Heart," and "Hand." *Soul* interpreters do it mostly out of love and compassion. These interpreters generally have Deaf family members. This group has interpreted most of their lives. They understand and know the Deaf culture, and really want Deaf people to understand the information relayed to them. They tend to go out of their way to clarify things that the Deaf do not easily understand. They realize the confusion and frustration of being Deaf because they have been exposed to deafness all their lives. *Heart* interpreters are people who love signing and sign language. They love the beauty and expressiveness of sign language and the Deaf culture. They truly want to relay information in a way so that the Deaf person can understand the culture of those who hear. Many times, *Heart* interpreters are found in churches. They do care about Deaf people, but sometimes they tend to regard us as needing "help" and "saving," rather than us needing communication assistance. *Heart* interpreters are sometimes uncomfortable in situations where the Deaf person uses profanity (yes, there is profanity in sign language), expresses anger, or uses sexual terms. *Hand* interpreters are in it for the money only. They just interpret, period. They do not take the time to know the Deaf consumers, or bother getting involved in Deaf events or being part of the Deaf culture. They just get certified, and then make money. This is not to say that interpreters do not need to earn a living, interpreters definitely need and deserve to earn a living for all that it takes to become certified. However, there are those few interpreters that get a reputation for being a *Hand*, who have no interest in our Deaf community, no interest in our Deaf culture, our Deaf history, and just do the minimum requirements. But, every business and every office has this type.

Just as the Deaf must deal with the different kinds of interpreters, interpreters must deal with the different kinds of Deaf/HH people; every Deaf/HH person has our own individual personality and background. An interpreter's job is to transmit information and communication to the Deaf person accurately and understandably, and do the same with information and communication expressed by the Deaf person. The interpreter must be able to recognize and adjust to the Deaf person's educational level, and interpret in a way with which the Deaf person understands. This is not easy! I have two stories that show just how hard it can be for an interpreter, and how difficult the English language can be to interpret:

> Back in the late 1970s, before there were professional interpreters available, I would sometimes try to help Deaf people by going to a doctor appointment with them and trying my best to lip-read the doctor, and then signing it to the Deaf person. However, sometimes the Deaf person I was helping had very little knowledge of spoken English. Some Deaf people did not understand that one English word can have several different meanings, or that certain words are a "Ten dollar word for a five-cent word." I remember the time I went with a HH woman to a doctor appointment and tried my best to help her communicate with her doctor. The doctor asked, "How well is your urination coming out." She looks at me puzzled and asked what did he mean"? I signed, "He wanted to know if you have problems going pee-pee?" She replied "no." Then he asked her how her stool was? She looked at me and said, "It is hard to sit on." At that point, I realized that she knew the word "stool" as having just one meaning. So I explained "The doctor wants to know how your poo-poo is?" Thankfully, we got through that doctor appointment alright.
>
> Another time, in the early 1980s, there was a Deaf man, Dale, who used to help me do gardening work and plant my annual vegetable garden. Dale was not educated, having grown up on a farm in the South, but he was a wonderful person and a reliable worker. Well, on this particular day, we ran out of fertilizer for the garden. So I sent Dale to the hardware store to get some more. He did not know what fertilizer was called. I told Dale to ask the

salesperson for "manure." Dale was unsure about what to ask for, so I finger spelled it for him: M-A-N-U-R-E. Poor Dale looked confused at the new word, so I said, "Think of man - u- are." Dale still looked at me very puzzled, so I repeated it a few times. I gave him money and told him to get five bags. Thirty minutes later, he was back unloading the manure. I asked if everything went okay, and he said he had a hard time with the salesman. At that point, he handed me the paper he wrote on. It read as follows:

Please 5 bag marue (crossed out)
Please 5 bag muare (crossed out)
Please 5 bag manare (crossed out)
Finally, he wrote: "Please 5 bag of cow shit"
He said the man laughed and laughed, and gave him the five bags.

While these stories above may be funny, they show how many Deaf/HH people do not have the access to language that people who hear do, and shows what I wrote earlier in the book about how you learn so much information through your hearing. Interpreting for someone like Dale requires a lot of skills. I have taught and mentored many interpreters, and really respect what is involved in the interpreting process. Because interpreters are the "ears and voices" for the Deaf/HH in a variety of situations, interpreting requires a strong knowledge of two languages and two cultures, and requires general knowledge of many different subjects. In some ways, being an interpreter is like dentistry or medicine. In dentistry and medicine, there is general practice, and then there are doctors who are specialists. When Deaf people receive intensive medical attention, they need interpreters who can not only sign and interpret all the terminology, but who can also handle the emotions that come with serious life and death situations. In schools, there are general education classes. However, there are times when interpreters are needed who have a background in Chemistry or Calculus. Many Deaf people today work for companies in Information Technology (IT), and those Deaf employees require interpreters who have knowledge of IT, and who can sign, interpret, and voice all the IT terminology. Interpreters who work in the courts must have a strong knowledge of legal vocabulary and be very familiar with the legal process. Another type of specialized interpreting is working with people who are both deaf and blind. There are also interpreters who specialize in theatrical interpreting. Video Relay Service (VRS) is another type of interpreting. You may be surprised to learn that there are also Deaf interpreters who interpret for Deaf consumers. They are called Certified Deaf Interpreters (CDI). CDIs are used mostly in legal and medical situations when a Deaf person does not have strong ASL abilities. These consumers may be from a foreign country, and not familiar with our language, or someone who did not go to school, has minimal language skills, and uses "home signs" and gestures. A CDI may also be needed when interpreting for a person who is developmentally disabled, or a deaf child that does not have strong language acquisition. Therefore, a team of both a hearing interpreter and a CDI would be used.

I am very lucky to live in Sacramento, California, where we have many professional sign language interpreters and specialized interpreting services. Many small towns throughout America do not have interpreting services available—forget about *specialized* interpreting services. Deaf people who live in these towns often still rely on family members, communicate by writing (assuming that the Deaf person understands written English) or they just get by on their own. This still happens very often, even though the ADA became law back in 1990.

Many Deaf/HH people have lived their entire lives getting by on their own. The growth in the number of interpreters does not mean that Deaf/HH people are unable to function without an interpreter. Many are fully able to function in everyday situations without any help. It is when we go to lectures, visit doctors, meet with lawyers, appear in court, attend plays, make telephone calls, or are in other situations when complete and accurate communication is vital, that an interpreter is needed. However, having access to interpreters is a wonderful thing.

Most Deaf people recognize that interpreting requires years of training. Yet, there are still a few Deaf people who gripe. Why is that? Some Deaf people do not know how much is involved with being a *professional* interpreter, and think it is just communicating in sign language. It could also be that a particular city has too many *Hand* interpreters, or mostly has interpreters who are not very skilled, and Deaf persons in that area are frustrated. Other areas may have a good balance of interpreters, with a large number of certified interpreters, and the Deaf persons in that city are quite happy. Griping is rare in areas with plenty of *Soul* and *Heart* interpreters. So, the differences in acceptance of the interpreting profession are understandable.

No matter what flaws or lack of understanding may exist, we Deaf/HH are much better off now. I feel a lot of love and respect for sign language interpreters. It is not easy to learn our language and culture, and all that comes with being a professional interpreter. I think a big reason for me having taught ASL and mentoring for nearly 40 years is mainly that I know many lives of Deaf/HH, like mine, are more comfortable and happy because of having access to the mainstream. That has changed many lives. So many more Deaf/HH students have been able to attend college and earn degrees, which led to more Deaf/HH people getting better jobs. Having interpreters available in the workplace, either for job interviews or staff meetings, led to many Deaf/HH people having more job satisfaction and feeling like a part of the team. Deaf/HH people are grateful—especially the older generations of Deaf people like me. My generation had "nothing." We remember the struggles. Sign language interpreters played a very important part in us breaking the sound barrier. I am no longer the "quiet person" I used to be. With an interpreter at my side, I am sometimes told to shut up!

"New technology has changed the world; however, what new technology has done for our families is ten times greater. Never again will the only choice for TV or movie watching be a foreign film with subtitles. Never again will a CODA have to walk home in the rain because the neighbor is not answering the phone to walk over and tell our Deaf parents we need a ride. The only bad thing about new technology is 'little devil CODAs' can no longer get away with mischief because school teachers and principals can now call Deaf parents on their videophones!"

Brian Diamond

Chapter 8

THE WONDERFUL WORLD OF TECHNOLOGY

Many people have said that the Information Technology revolution was as important to the history and development of the late 1900s as the Industrial Revolution was to the late 1800s. The government, Wall Street, or the common person who shops at Wal-Mart—no one can deny all the benefits of technology. However, for me and other people who do not hear, modern technologies changed our lives *even more*—and moved us forward into "equality" for the first time in history.

Being deaf traditionally meant being shut off from communication, spoken language, and society in general. Technology enabled us to become a part of the mainstream. Starting with the TTY, relay services, captioned television programs, the Internet, two-way pagers, video relay service and videophones, and new gadgets that pop up every few months, technology has almost eliminated this isolation and allowed us to become a part of society, part of our families, and to obtain high-skill professional jobs.

Things that many people take for granted, making a phone call to a family member, leaving a message on a voicemail, checking your own messages on your voicemail, enjoying a movie at the theater, knowing what is being said on television shows—including emergency warnings on the news—was just not possible for more than half of my life. My own children did not realize the struggle I went through before modern technology. It was when my children were older and understood about deafness that they asked me "Mom, how did you get by back then with 'nothing'?" I told them "I don't know, but I did. I was able to get through extreme hardships. But I am not the only one. Many of my Deaf friends also shared the same experiences."

A TELEPHONE FOR THE DEAF

Alexander Graham Bell stumbling upon the telephone while trying to invent a device to help his deaf wife and his deaf mother to hear, is a well-known story in the Deaf community. Before Bell's telephone, Americans used the Western Union Telegraph system that sent Morse code through telegraph keys, to send and receive messages. Western Union and AT&T later switched to teletype machines (TTYs), which used a typewriter-like keyboard to send typed messages instead of Morse code. In 1964, Robert Weitbrecht, a brilliant deaf physicist from California (yes, a deaf physicist), invented the acoustic coupler (a cradle for the telephone) which converted the tones/codes made by TTYs into typed messages that could be sent and received through the household telephone. As the story goes, Weitbrecht worked with the old TTY machines Western Union and AT&T had lying around, to try to come up with a way to communicate through the telephone with his friend who was also deaf. When Weitbrecht invented the acoustic coupler, telephone companies fought against the idea of using it with their equipment (this history is told in a wonderful book "A Phone of Our Own" by Dr. Harry Lang - Gallaudet Press), so a phone for deaf people was blocked.

From what I understand, TTYs did become available by the late 1960s, but they had to be paid for. At that time, very few deaf and hard of hearing people could afford TTYs, or even knew about them (I know that I did not find out about TTYs until the late 1970s). Fortunately for us, the Rehabilitation Act of 1973 required providing reasonable accommodations for persons or employees with disabilities. But, it was not until 1978 that the telephone part of the law really took effect, and when TTYs were provided to people who were deaf or hard of hearing. Almost overnight, TTYs became common in the deaf and hard of hearing world. Now, for the first time, a deaf person could call another deaf person and carry on a conversation over telephone lines! I remember this creating a wave of excitement in our community, a lot like the one that swept the hearing world with the invention of the telephone. Blinking lights, (the signal for a ringing telephone) had every person in a deaf household rushing to the TTY to see who was calling. Deaf people who lived in that era will remember spending day and night doing nothing but having typed conversations with Deaf friends through the telephone for hours and hours. The experience was just too thrilling to let everyday responsibilities interfere! Yes, I was one of those people. Having a TTY now meant that if I wanted to talk to one of my Deaf friends, I no longer had to drive across town to their house. Now, I could *call* them to see if they were home!

I remember the first TTYs were almost the size of a mailbox, and green—like military mailboxes. Just like computers and cell phones that started out big and bulky, and got smaller with advancing technology, TTYs also became smaller over time. We Deaf look back now on those first TTYs and laugh. We refer to them as the "green monsters." Even before the big TTYs became widely used, some individuals and companies were already working on smaller, portable versions of the TTY. A portable TTY was actually first shown at the California Association for the Deaf (CAD) convention in Sacramento in 1973. In my Preface of this book, I talked about when I worked at NorCal Center on Deafness (now NorCal Services for the Deaf and Hard of Hearing) in 1980 and a gentleman walked in with a much smaller version of the TTY, called the TDD (Telephone Device for the Deaf). It was a modern style of the portable TTY that was first introduced years earlier. That meeting at NorCal led to Deaf leaders in the Sacramento area to try to convince the California legislature to make TDD's affordable to deaf and hard of hearing persons (at the time they had to be rented for $30 a month—a lot of money in 1980). This grass roots movement resulted in the first laws in the nation requiring local telephone companies to provide deaf customers with free TDD's and special rates for their telephone bills (because a typed conversation required many more minutes than a spoken conversation).

THE TTY RELAY SERVICE

TTY/TDD conversations only took place when two people both had either a TTY/TDD. But what if a deaf person wanted to call a hearing person, or business that did not have one? *If a deaf person with a TTY called a person who hears who had a TTY, and that hearing person called another hearing person or business and relayed the typed message from the deaf person, then relayed what the hearing person said back to the deaf person, a successful conversation could happen.* Around 1974, these were the thoughts of several people at Converse Communications of Connecticut, the first Deaf and Hard of Hearing service center to establish TTY relay services. In the next year or two, Communication Services for the Deaf in South Dakota began TTY relay services. In 1981, Deaf leaders at CAD, NorCal, and other Deaf Service Centers in California worked together to create a relay service center in Sacramento. Several more relay centers later appeared in California; then a few opened in other states. Fortunately, in 1987, California passed a law requiring funding for Telecommunications Relay Services (TRS). Ironically, AT&T, one of the companies that fought against using their equipment when Robert Weitbrecht first invented the acoustic coupler, led that program. Over the next few years relay centers being to pop up across the country, but were still not available in many states. When the ADA passed in 1990, it required TRS be available in all 50 states, 24 hours a day, seven days a week. We were all very excited about this; however, it took several years to get set up in all 50 states. Relay services allowed me and other Deaf people to call our hearing family members, hearing friends, make doctor appointments, and do usual business, just like hearing people. Can you imagine the impact this had on us? Many people might have taken this for granted because people who hear had been using the telephone in this way for almost 100 years. But, for me and almost every other deaf person, this was life changing! It was the beginning of us finally breaking into the world of those who hear instead of being isolated amongst our own people and ourselves. During this era, we started to become somewhat independent. We could now call and communicate on a one-to-one basis and not have to depend on our children or our neighbors to make telephone calls for us. We could order pizza deliveries and Chinese takeout for the first time ever! It was just so exciting for us to do these kinds of things by ourselves for the very first time!

The relay service was available to both deaf and hearing people through an 800 number where deaf persons could call hearing persons and hearing persons could call deaf persons. The service was free to the caller, but long-distance charges still applied; however, in 2001, the 800 number was replaced nationwide by dialing 711. Relay Operators functioned in the same way as sign language interpreters—they voiced the deaf person's typed words to the person who hears, then typed the person who hears spoken words back to the deaf person.

Although this was wonderful, after a while, some people got tired of the time consuming process it took to do a TTY relay call. Some people that hear, who had deaf friends or deaf family members, would buy a TDD of their own so they could communicate faster (just like people becoming impatient with dial-up Internet service and buying high-speed Internet service). By that time, many companies were making TDDs and they were much cheaper than when they first came out.

I must point out that even though the term "TDD" was now being used by hearing people, many Deaf people still called them TTYs. The reason was the term "TDD" was created by Pacific Bell, the company established by Alexander Graham Bell. Because of Alexander Graham Bell's association with eugenics and his oppression of Deaf people and Deaf culture, most everyone in the Deaf community continued to use the term "TTY." This is the reason you may see "TTY/TDD" where there is a separate Voice and TTY/TDD line.

While the relay service was life changing for us, relay calls to businesses and other people who hear was not always greeted with open arms. Actually, some of those who received relay calls were rude to the relay operator, and would make insulting asides to fellow workers, or other present people who hear, while talking on the line. What the hearing person on the other end did not know was that relay operators are trained and required to inform the deaf person of all sounds that they hear (yes, many of us "heard" the cuss words spoken when someone who hears was "stuck" with a relay call). Many businesses were probably not aware that impatient, inconsiderate employees cost them deaf customers. Using the TTY relay system is not difficult, it is just a bit time consuming to go through a third person to read the typed words and then relay it. All it requires is speaking clearly enough for the relay operator to type what is being said, to say "GA" when finished with what you are saying, and "SK" when ending the call (this means "Go Ahead" and "Stop Keying" and is from the old Western Union telegraphs). This was a small inconvenience, yet unfortunately, many people who hear did not gladly accept it.

Very few of us have a TTY in our homes today. Modern times moved almost all of us into faster and more streamlined video relay services (VRS). The handful of us who choose to keep a TTY today, still have to deal with impatient and rude people on the other end of the phone, but I do not believe it is as bad as it used to be.

CAPTIONED TELEVISION AND MOVIES:

In Chapter 6, I wrote about closed-captioning providing large amounts of missing information to those of us who do not hear. I wrote, "TV without closed-captions is like a hearing person watching TV with the sound turned off." Before closed-captioning, very few of us watched TV—unless it was something very expressive and physical like "I Love Lucy," "The Carol Burnett Show," old slapstick comedies, or sports. Movies? Forget it. Hardly any one of us went to the movies unless it was something visually exciting like the James Bond thrillers.

Closed-captioning was termed "closed" because a special converter had to be attached to the television set to receive the captioning. It was expensive to own one, so not all of us had the "black boxes." In the 1970s, we had some closed-captioning on a limited basis, maybe five percent of all the programs on television. But, we were glad to have those because previously we had NOTHING. Some of us older Deaf remember in the early 1980s that two of the programs that were closed-captioned were "Dynasty" and "Dallas." It may seem silly now, but that was an historic time for us. For the first time, Deaf people were ***hearing*** how "rich hearing people spoke and lived." For the first time, Deaf people were enjoying soap operas and following the developing story lines. Deaf people would clear out their schedules and make sure they were home on the nights "Dynasty" and "Dallas" came on. Deaf people knew better than to call someone on the TTY on those nights! The next day at work, Deaf people could be a part of the "water cooler" talk. Deaf people seldom were a part of "water cooler" talk sessions before this. By the end of the 1980s, maybe thirty percent of all programs were closed-captioned. The Americans with Disabilities Act changed that, thanks largely to Congressman Tom Harkin of Iowa. Harkin is an advocate for people with disabilities, and he introduced the ADA to Congress. Harkin had a brother who was Deaf, and he delivered part of his speech in sign language so his brother could understand. The ADA required captioning for all programs and movies shown on TV. The ADA also required that all new television sets to have built-in captioning capability. Now the word "closed" no longer applied. However, to this day, some television listings still use the initials "CC" to show that a program is captioned.

Around 1995, after all programs on television became captioned, a little bit of controversy came out over which programs should or should not be captioned. I remember reading about how critics argued that the millions of dollars the U.S. Department of Education claimed to spend each year for captioning would be better spent if some programs were not captioned. The USA Today published a letter from a reader who said way too much money was spent on captioning, and that captioning programs like <u>The Jerry Springer Show</u> and <u>Maury Povich</u> were a waste of taxpayer's money. My son Brian read this and wrote a letter in rebuttal. He said in part:

> "...if you do not hear the radio, the TV, or the conversations of others, how would you know of breaking news? Most people do not realize how much they are informed through their hearing. Since the development of captioning a few years ago, my parents, along with other deaf people, know what is being said on CNN and get access to world news. Many Americans get their political views from hearing what is said on the late night talk shows. My parents never had that advantage. Now, they get to "hear" the political jokes told by Jay Leno and David Letterman during their monologues. My parents and their Deaf friends now know what is being said in Academy Award winning movies. Deaf people are now more in tune with pop culture and Americana than ever before because programming like MTV is captioned. While you and I may completely agree that shows like 'Jerry Springer' and 'Maury Povich' are dysfunctional garbage, we have arrived at this conclusion because we can HEAR what is being said on these programs."

Fortunately, the FCC required all programs on TV to be captioned. The ADA and FCC stressed "functional equivalence" with television, meaning deaf persons have the equivalent right to watch any program they choose to watch in the same way as those who hear. Whether it was trashy nonsense or a religious program, deaf persons now had the equal right to watch the show or change the channel, just like persons who hear.

Closed-captioning gave me and other deaf people a form of entertainment we never fully had. It brought families and friends together to share a common enjoyment. Deaf parents with hearing children usually had to watch action programs and movies. It did not always bring the family together because of the limited choices that might not be of common interest to everyone. Now, having all the captioned movie choices gave me and my family great nights where we could all sit together, eat popcorn, and bond as a family. The same goes for Deaf friends who gather. We could make snacks, have a beer, and enjoy a movie or TV show.

Movies produced after 1994, and available for rent in the video stores, were also required by the ADA to be captioned. You cannot imagine what this did for deaf and hard of hearing people. We now had an entertainment option to stay home and rent a video like those who hear had been doing for the past 10 years. Still, going to the local theater to see the latest film was not the same experience for us, because movies in the theaters were not captioned. So, we had to wait for the movie to come out on VHS or DVD.

In the late 1990s through the 2000s, there were a handful of theaters across the country that had one night a month where they would show a movie with captions. About 2013, there was an amendment to the ADA, requiring all movie theaters to provide closed captioning and audio description for customers with hearing and vision disabilities. It took a few years to work out the technology, but today there are small, portable screens that attach to the cup holder in the theater seat, which show captions on a LED display. These mini boxes have visors around the screen so it does not distract other movie customers. There is also "invisible captions" technology that are along the bottom of movie screens, which can only be seen when wearing special 3-D type glasses. There are also special captioning glasses that work on the theater's Wi-Fi system. When a deaf/hard of hearing person wears these glasses, a small projector shows the captions on the glasses, which can only be seen by the person wearing them. In Sacramento, we have several theaters that have this equipment. I have gone to the movies and used two types of these captioning devices, and I just cannot tell you how exciting it has been to go see Disney movies with my grandkids. There are movie theaters in bigger cities across the country that use this equipment now, but not all movie theaters, as there is always a long delay with a new law and it fully going into effect. At the time of this writing, I am sure there are many more cities and towns that do not have this equipment than those that do.

COMPUTERS AND THE INTERNET

In the 1990s, the Internet began to change the way Americans received information and communicated. For deaf people who had been deprived of information for so long, the Internet brought us major change. Closed-captioning on television brought access to news, language, music, comedy, and pop culture to deaf people; now the Internet brought it much, much more. Yes, the Internet changed the lives of people who hear. However, before the Internet, people who hear were able to receive information by listening to the radio in their cars. They also had sound on every station and every program on their television for their entire lives. People who hear also picked up information by just hearing other people speak, or by talking with strangers at the grocery store. The Internet was just so helpful and informative to those of us who are deaf. When a movie or TV program is captioned, a lot of time is spent on getting the captions correct before it is released. But when the news is captioned, it is being typed at the same time it is spoken, and I always see many errors in the spelling, or that big pieces of information are left out. The Internet now allowed us to get a news story, with pictures, explanations, and opinions. The Internet, in some ways, gave to deaf persons what talk radio gave to persons who hear.

For most Americans, e-mails are a part of our daily routine and make communication easier. But for deaf people, when e-mail first became popular, it turned out to be the way to get an important message to another deaf person. Although we had TTYs at the time, TTYs did not have answering machines (until later models). Unlike hearing people who had been leaving messages on voice mails for years, we could not leave a message for someone who was not home, or had missed the call. Deaf people had to keep calling repeatedly. I can remember how many times I would have to drive over to another deaf person's home and leave a note on their door.

People who have specialty interests, or make up a small percentage of the population, have found similar people or groups on the Internet. For us, there is information on Deaf organizations, Deaf services, and Deaf social gatherings. Deaf people put videos on YouTube and Facebook in sign language, all about new technology for deaf and hard of hearing people, or important issues in the Deaf community. There are comedy videos on YouTube and Facebook by Deaf people, or children of Deaf adults, on issues that are funny specifically to the Deaf community. There are even Deaf chat rooms and Deaf dating websites to meet Deaf singles (no, at my age, I am not visiting any Deaf dating websites). The Internet has all but eliminated the isolation that came with being deaf, given us a lot of the information we always missed, and brought us into the mainstream.

PAGERS / TEXTING DEVICES

When pagers first came out in the 1990s, you could only enter a phone number for the person to call back. People who hear could call the number entered on the pager, but for people who do not hear, there was little benefit from pagers (going to a pay phone to call that number was not so easy for us). Later, pagers with two-way texting came out. People who were deaf or hard of hearing could now send and receive text messages. The new two-way pagers allowed us to contact our family or friends. They allowed us to contact people when we were downtown, at the mall, the grocery store, or stuck on a dark roadside somewhere with a car problem.

When two-way texting devices became very popular with people who hear, I could not understand why. I figured *"You have a cell phone where you can TALK to other hearing people. Why would you send a text message?"* For people who hear, sending text messages back and forth to each other should have seemed like they were stepping back into the old days of sending Morse code or a telegram.

One thing I had to learn about was the alert when a text message came in. The beeping option instead of the vibrating option caused some annoyed stares from those who could hear it! Sorry folks, I didn't know!

While some people who hear do not have a cell phone or other mobile electronic devices, it is almost impossible to find a deaf person who does not have one. Besides all the same reasons that hearing people have them (Internet, e-mail, GPS, etc.) deaf people need them for roadside, as well as other emergencies. As of this writing, most highway roadside service boxes are still not accessible to those who cannot hear. Today, most deaf/hard of hearing people have mobile videophones or smartphones that allow them to connect to a video relay interpreter to call 911. But for me, I am of the older generation, and l do not have a mobile videophone or smartphone.

VIDEOPHONES AND VIDEO RELAY SERVICE

A long time ago, people, hearing and deaf, used to wonder if there would come a day in the future when you would be able to see the person you are talking to on the phone. My kids used to talk about that when they watched the "Jetsons," a cartoon about life in the future where they had telephones with monitors and people could see each other.

Ed Bosson is known as "The Father of Video Relay Service," and is a hero in the Deaf community. A Deaf graduate of Gallaudet University, he is responsible for the Video Relay Service (VRS) that greatly changed my life, and the lives of many who are Deaf or hard of hearing. In the early 1990s when the Internet and web-cams came out, he had an idea to team a sign language interpreter with a web-cam to communicate in sign language with a deaf or hard of hearing person who were also using a web-cam. Bosson's idea was to do relay services in sign language through the Internet like how TTY relay services were being done through the telephone for the last 20 years. He presented his idea to several employees at the Texas Sprint Relay to see if it was possible. After many more video and Internet tests in several cities in Texas, and confirming that the FCC would allow funding for this type of relay service, VRS was born!

Around 2000, Communication Services for the Deaf (CSD) in Sioux Falls, South Dakota (the same center that was one of the first to offer TTY relay services) got involved. They set up VRS in Texas and then in South Dakota. This was all new, and it took time to establish VRS centers and improve the technology. CSD formed a partnership with a company called Sorenson. They created the videophone, a web-cam device that immediately connects a Deaf or hard of hearing caller to a Video Interpreter (VI). The VI appears on our TV screen or computer monitor through the Internet, and they will call the number we request and interpret the conversation between us and the hearing person we are calling. I cannot tell you how much this changed my life, and the lives of Deaf people like me. When making a call through the videophone, the VI calls the business or person and explains that this is a VRS call, they tell them how it will work, and then voice relays the Deaf person's signing to the hearing person. The VI, in return, signs back to the Deaf person what the person who hears is saying. The conversation is the same as you would communicate as if you were using TTY relay service, however, there is no "GA" or "SK" needed in these conversations. VRS conversations are so much faster and feel more like a natural conversation than with TTY relay. The VIs are trained to relay the Deaf person's communication and remain "invisible," making it appear that the person on the line is "talking" for themselves.

Within a few years, many companies began to offer VRS nationwide. By 2006, the FCC passed a law that required VRS be available 24 hours a day, seven days a week (in the "functionally equivalent" way telephones are available for those who hear).

Videophones do not have to be used with an interpreter only. Videophones also have an option to communicate directly with another Deaf person where me and my Deaf friends can see each other and sign to one another. Talking to my Deaf friends and seeing them on my TV screen is an amazing and fascinating experience! One of the most fun things I have done in my life was when I got my first videophone and called some of my old classmates from Gallaudet University. It was like flying across the country and seeing them in person! With videophones, we can "visit" our family and friends right in our living room! Then, I called old childhood classmates ("brothers and sisters") from the Berkeley School for the Deaf (now located in Fremont, CA) that I had not seen in years. Later, I called long lost hearing friends through the VRS. It was funny because, at first, some of them thought I suddenly had my hearing back! I said "No, I am calling through a person who hears." I had to explain that this was new technology that I am using.

A long lost hearing friend of mine was very ill and dying of cancer. I found her through some friends and called her. We had a good talk; not as long as I would have liked, due to her limited energy, but she was so excited and happy to talk with me. She made me promise to call her again soon. I told her I surely would. However, two days later when I called again, she had already passed away. I was so very grateful to have had this communication with her before she left for her journey. My heart was full of gratitude. I would not have this satisfaction without VRS. Thank you, Ed Bosson. Thank you.

Today, the deaf and hard of hearing are "equal" to those who hear, and have the independence of calling anyone we want. Today, we can call anywhere in the world through the interpreter on our screen. VRS allows us to call any country (in addition to English and sign language, VIs are also available to speak Spanish). Because of VRS, I and Deaf/hard of hearing people make important business calls to our lawyer, stockbroker, doctor etc. and not worry about taking up so much of their time. We know the phone call will be almost the same as when two hearing people talk on the phone. Although we did and do appreciate TTY relay services, VRS is like having an actual interpreter right there in the room with you. VRS has brought family members together that did not communicate with each other much before. I cannot tell you how much I enjoy talking with my grandkids through VRS.

Some Deaf people told me VRS helped them to communicate with their parents for the FIRST time! Sadly, some of the conversations were not pleasant. They "hollered" at their parents through the VRS because their parents never cared or took the time to learn sign language and communicate with their child. Until now, they had no way of telling their parents how they felt.

Before VRS, many deaf kids in the mainstream schools were just considered "the deaf kid or kids that sat in the front." Hearing classmates ignored them. Now, they communicate all the time with their classmates through the VRS. Deaf parents can now communicate with their child's teachers and be kept up to date on their child's progress. Never before could they do this unless they set up a meeting, arranged an interpreter, drove to the school, etc. It all used to be so time consuming and frustrating. Back when my kids were in school, my son had to interpret a Parent/Teacher conference. That was not my choice, but it was the 1970s, and it was my only choice.

As wonderful as VRS is, some Deaf people still prefer the old method of the TTY/TDDs because they don't like to look at an interpreter on the screen and share personal information, even though the VIs keep everything strictly confidential. The other reason is that some people just do not like new technology.

ASSISTIVE DEVICES

Going back to the 1960s, long before the Information Technology Revolution, we had assistive devices to alert us of things around the house that we did not hear. When I had my kids in the 1960s, we had signal lights to let us know when the baby was crying. We had doorbell lights to let us know when someone was at the door. In the 1970s when we got TTYs, we had lights to notify us that the telephone was ringing. In the 1980s, we had fire alarms with lights to warn us of a fire. Somewhere along the way, we got alarm clocks with flashing lights (although some alarm clocks are put under your pillow because they vibrate). Even with the advances in technology, all the "old classics" are still around today. You may wonder if all the flashing lights make our homes glitter like the Las Vegas Strip. In reality, how often does someone come to the door? Twice a week? How often does your phone ring under normal circumstances? A few times a day? So, no, our homes do not light up like a Christmas tree. But if your fire alarm ever flashes more than once, that's a problem! Each of our assistive devices in our homes has a different type of flashing light; we identify which one it is and absorb the information.

NEW GADGETS

It is not possible to list all of the devices available today that have helped us to become independent and on the same level with those who hear. As I write this, it seems there is some new gadget coming out almost every 20 minutes. I have listed the main technologies that have greatly improved our lives. However, there are two more wonderful inventions I should mention: captioned telephones and mobile videophones.

Captioned telephones are for deaf or hard of hearing persons who do not use sign language. These may be people who lost their hearing later in life, or grew up using the oral method. Individuals using captioned telephones speak for themselves and have what is said back to them delivered in captions. It requires being connected to a PC, tablet, or smartphone. A call box will appear and the deaf or hard of hearing person enters the telephone number they want to call, and then enters the number they want the captioning service to call them on (connected to their phone or PC). This will automatically connect to the captioning service first, and then connect to the person or business being called. When the other party answers, everything the other party says is captioned and displayed on the PC or phone.

Mobile videophones are just that—videophones that are mobile. They are battery operated, have Wi-Fi capability, or run on an Internet connection. You can talk to another person who has a videophone, or use it to make a call using VRS. You can use it at home, or use it anywhere there is a Wi-Fi connection. Mobile videophones are cell phones for the Deaf!

Years ago, if someone had told me that one day I would see commercials and programs with sign language, be able to watch captioned television and movies, and be able to make telephone calls just like those who can hear, I would have thought they were crazy! Who would have dreamed that after being isolated and closed out of the world for so long, me and the older Deaf would move into the mainstream of society?! Deaf kids today have it much better than Deaf people my age did. We older Deaf people now have our own "When I was your age, I walked barefoot in the snow, uphill both ways" stories to tell the younger Deaf generations!

"In terms of a disability, I do not view myself as having a disability …
I function like any other hearing person can. My deafness does not
deprive me of anything. I can do anything I want. Except maybe sing."

Summer Crider, University of Texas at Austin

Chapter 9

THE WORKPLACE

Until the mid-1990s, the ways of making a living were very limited for Deaf/HH people. Equal access, better communication, becoming part of the mainstream, and independence are all results of the Rehabilitation Act, the Americans with Disabilities Act, the rise in sign language interpreters, and modern technology. All of those things combined led to major changes in employment opportunities for us. Today, people who do not hear make a living as doctors, dentists, computer programmers, software engineers, actors in film and television, accountants, insurance agents, investment advisors, college professors and more. Even many Deaf employees work at the Pentagon!

The period before the ADA and modern technology were the "Dark Ages," because there were so few occupations available. Some of us were able to get menial jobs as janitors or dishwashers. Those of us who were lucky enough to find skilled work were mostly printers or keypunch data operators. Some Deaf men found jobs working in bakeries. Skilled Deaf women typists could maybe get a file clerk position. If we were lucky enough to attend Gallaudet College (College back then, University today) and get our degree, we could become teachers in one of the Deaf residential schools across the nation. Deaf people like myself did not go "job hunting" because very few companies would hire us. Many of us, including myself, went to the Department of Vocational Rehabilitation for help to get a job. I was one of the fortunate Deaf people to get a job as a keypunch data operator. Once I got a job, I had to force myself to work harder than all the other employees, being the first one to show up in the mornings, the first one back from the coffee breaks, the last one to leave every day. I wanted to give a good impression. This was so that my boss would tell my Vocational Rehabilitation counselor that Deaf people are good workers, hopefully encouraging the Department of Vocational Rehabilitation to send more Deaf people out into the field to become employed. While I was happy to have a job, I hated to check my wrist watch all the time to make sure I was the first back from breaks, or working all the way to the end of the day. Employees who hear would always be talking and laughing, taking their time to get to their desks and start working, or stopping work early. They were not stressed like I was every day. Getting a good job and being steadily employed often depended upon the compassion of good-hearted employers. The following anecdote, told to me by a Deaf man, demonstrates my point:

> Jack woke up at 4 a.m., put on his running attire, and hung his dress clothes in his car. He drove to the building of prospective employment, parked his old beat up car, and walked to a nearby donut shop. While walking, he picked up a section of yesterday's newspaper that someone threw away. Jack sat in the donut shop reading the tattered newspaper, drinking coffee and killing time. Eventually, he went into the restroom to change into his dress clothes. Jack wanted to be the *very first* person in line for the job interview (in those days, employers talked with potential employees and would decide whether to hire them; you actually spoke with someone—you did not fax or e-mail a resume). Jack had six years of experience in the specific line of work he was applying for. Unfortunately, he did not get the job. A hearing person with no experience was hired. Jack told me with some bitterness that he knew it was because the employer did not want to bother with having to write back and forth, or deal with an employee who could not hear.

During this time, working as a printer was the most common job for Deaf men. Printing companies and newspapers were always willing to hire deaf persons, as many who could hear did not want that kind of work. This was because the old printing equipment was very, very loud. Of course, it did not bother those who could not hear! My husband worked as a printer, while I was a keypunch operator in the 1960s and 1970s. Keypunching was repetitive work. Employees who hear listened to radios or communicated with other employees to break up the boredom. For me, I was just glad to have a job.

Today, with the equal access federal and state laws, and the luxury of the Internet providing huge amounts of information at the touch of a button, it may be hard to understand that not so long ago we could never imagine that one day Deaf people would have career options—just like those who hear. Before having communication and information instantly available on a mobile device or personal computer, the Deaf helped each other with news of job opportunities. There were many Deaf clubs back then, and we met weekly to discuss possible leads, who to contact, where to go etc. We had no videophones, mobile devices, or TTYs, so information had to be gathered at the Deaf clubs. On those Friday and Saturday nights, the men hung out over a beer to discuss job prospects. The women huddled together to discuss children, cooking, and a possible job opening.

In addition to getting help finding jobs at Deaf clubs, the Deaf also opened their home to Deaf travelers—those who might be in town for a prospective job. While it may sound strange to some, it was not uncommon back then for a Deaf stranger to just show up and ask to use the shower or to stay overnight. I know this sounds weird, but back then, we helped each other survive in a world where we were shut out. Before iPhones, video phones, texting devices, or access to a TTY, the Deaf just welcomed their "kin" into their home without any advance notice. We stuck together. We had to. Most Deaf people could not get help from their own families— most had hearing families who did not even sign. Employment agencies only assisted those who could hear. Centers for the Deaf did not really exist back then.

Many employers did not want to take a chance on a worker who could not hear, or they were afraid to. What most employers did not know is that Deaf persons were likely to work harder and miss less work than workers who could hear. This was mainly because Deaf persons *greatly* appreciated their jobs. Opportunities were so few for us, and when we were lucky enough to land a job, we did everything to keep it. Because very few hearing people knew sign language, spending a lot of idle time talking with other employees did not happen—making Deaf workers more productive. Also, calling in sick when you were Deaf was not as easy as it was for employees who could hear. We did not have the advantage of being able to pick up a telephone and call in sick, or to inform our employer that our child was ill. It was difficult to have to ask a hearing neighbor or friend call for us at 6:00 am. It was also embarrassing. Furthermore, a misunderstanding or miscommunication about missing work could result in the catastrophe of being fired. So, Deaf employees would rarely miss a day or take time off, even if it caused them a lot of stress and possible pain.

It was also during these "Dark Ages" when there was the way of life of Deaf peddlers. All across the nation, Deaf peddlers were common in cities large and small. They thrived wherever an innocent public whose pity had been stirred would give them money or purchase their alphabet cards, or a cheap trinket of some type. Because of vagrancy or trespassing laws, many Deaf peddlers were arrested. Sadly, many were thrown in jail without interpreters or explanations. Most communications were in writing, and many of those peddlers, being uneducated, could barely, if at all, read English (remember ASL is not English). Without an interpreter or clear communication, they were forced out of town.

A disturbing part of peddling was the way in which manipulative Deaf persons, who were "Kingpins," took advantage of some Deaf persons with a lack of education and poor communication abilities, or those with multiple disabilities. The Kingpins were more educated than the peddlers they used on the streets. They led groups that usually traveled a circuit—in order to cover as much ground as possible and to expose themselves to more unsuspecting people. The Kingpins were purely interested in lining their own pockets rather than in helping their recruited Deaf members. Each member might have to go out begging on a daily basis with a quota that they were expected to meet in the amount of money they should bring in. If they failed to earn enough, the angry Kingpin might deprive them of food and other necessities as punishment, or even physically abuse them. The peddler usually received little or none of the money they brought in each day. Because the peddlers lacked the necessary skills to hold down real jobs, lacked the communication abilities to report the abuse that was happening to them, or lacked the support of a family, they would rarely attempt to break away. The situation was very much like slavery.

During this period in the 1960s–1970s, members of the Deaf community who had jobs and families hated Deaf peddlers because it gave society the impression that peddling was the only thing Deaf people were capable of doing. Even today, many people in society are still unaware of the great changes and advances that have taken place in the workplace for the Deaf. Although Deaf peddlers are mostly outdated, there are still a few peddlers here and there. The Deaf community, now more than ever, feel that peddlers reinforce a negative stereotype—and set Deaf people back 30 years. Yes, there is still the occasional Deaf person who is a peddler, and there always will be. But, just like a hearing person on an off ramp with a sign that says, "I Will Work For Food" or a person who hears that is on the street asking for spare change does not represent hearing people as a whole, Deaf peddlers do not represent Deaf people as a whole. A certain part of the population of people who hear have drug or alcohol problems, are illiterate, or suffer from mental illness. The same can be said for a certain part of the population of Deaf people.

It is sometimes hard for me to believe the incredible changes that I have seen over the last 30 years in the lives of those who are Deaf/HH. It began with enlightened legislators throughout the country passing laws, or providing funding for Community Service Agencies that specifically served Deaf persons. These agencies provided a range of services that had never been available to Deaf persons, such as counseling services, referral services, interpreting services, job training, employment placement, and other services. Of course, the passage of the ADA was the single greatest law that led to changes in employment opportunities for the Deaf/HH, and in the workplace. Employers could no longer discriminate against applicants or employees with disabilities. The ADA emphasized "equal access" and "functional equivalence," and that directly led to the growth in sign language interpreters and interpreting services. Now, many more Deaf/HH persons could attend colleges, workshops, and other educational trainings. Better education led to more jobs, better jobs, and higher paying jobs. Sign language interpreters reduced the communication barrier in job interviews. The Internet and other wonderful new technology helped us to find out about job possibilities, apply, and set up job interviews—which

I could have never imagined on those Friday and Saturday nights at the Deaf club!

So much progress has been made for the Deaf/HH in the workplace that it is shocking for some people to learn that we now have many of the same occupations once held only by those who hear. In the workplace today there are Deaf/deaf **doctors**, Deaf/deaf **lawyers**, Deaf/deaf **dentists**, Deaf/deaf **psychologists**, Deaf/deaf **financial advisors**, Deaf/deaf **insurance agents**, Deaf/deaf **computer programmers**, Deaf/deaf **engineers**, Deaf/deaf **biologists**, Deaf/deaf **laboratory technicians**, Deaf/deaf **actors**, Deaf/deaf **professional athletes** (Curtis Pride played for the Boston Red Sox and the New York Yankees and the Anaheim Angels, and Derrick Coleman played for the Seattle Seahawks), Deaf/deaf **athletic trainers**, Deaf/deaf **administrators**, and more. Several Deaf/deaf people across the country own their own businesses. Many Deaf/deaf people have **PhDs**. I should also mention that there are Deaf/deaf **authors**!

Some of the Deaf professionals I mention, I have met personally. A Deaf doctor works at the University of California Davis Medical Center in Sacramento, and has two interpreters that he works with when seeing patients. The interpreters stand behind a glass shield when the doctor is working on a surgery team. I have dined at Mozzeria, a restaurant in San Francisco owned and operated by two Deaf persons that attended Gallaudet University. Mozzeria, which has mostly Deaf employees and a few hearing employees who sign, has been featured in many news articles, including the *New York Times*, and has won numerous awards for restaurant excellence. A Deaf man here in Sacramento, who has done work on my house, owns a construction business. He started out as an apprentice, but later went to school and earned a degree in business, then set up his own construction business. I have two Deaf friends here in Sacramento also, who are government employees working for the State of California as computer programmers, and one more as an Accounting Administrator. Another Deaf friend of mine in Sacramento is a licensed Marriage and Family Therapist, who got her Master's Degree in Counseling from Gallaudet, and then received a Master's Degree in Social/Clinical in San Francisco. While these professionals are in Northern California, there are many other Deaf/deaf business owners, doctors, dentists, chefs, fashion designers, art directors, and more, all across the United States.

Breaking the Sound Barrier

There seems to be no limit to what the Deaf of today's generation can do in the performing arts. In the 21st century, we have a Deaf musician/rapper, Sean Forbes (he has several videos on the Internet). I do not mean a musician who has hearing problems or is hard of hearing, but a person who is who is profoundly deaf, has been deaf since he was an infant, attended National Technological Institute for the Deaf (NTID), and uses ASL. Sean Forbes is a rapper who has worked with the same record producers who have worked with Eminem. We had a Deaf MMA/UFC fighter, Matt "The Hammer" Hamill, who was the subject of the movie "The Hammer." Russell Harvard, the Deaf actor who played Matt Hamill in "The Hammer," has appeared in several movies, including "There Will Be Blood," which won an Academy Award and several other awards. Shoshanna Stern, a beautiful and talented Deaf actress, who was also in "The Hammer," has appeared in several movies and several television series. We have a Deaf film director, Mark Wood, who is the co-founder of a production company that has made several feature films. Wood's movies star Deaf actors/actresses who sign throughout the movie. The movies are a "reverse method," where they are captioned for viewers who do not understand sign language. David H. Pierce, who attended NTID, is a film and television producer, and the owner of Davideo Productions in Seguin, Texas. There have also been Deaf people who have appeared on Reality TV shows such as: "Project Runway," "Chopped," and "The Amazing Race." Several Deaf people have been contestants on "The Price is Right." Deaf people appearing on Reality TV shows began with Christy Smith, a graduate of Gallaudet University, who became a contestant on "Survivor" back in 2003. Christy was billed as "the first disabled Survivor contestant." In 2015, Nyle DiMarco won on "America's Next Top Model," and followed that in 2016 by appearing on "Dancing with the Stars." I am so amazed at what I have seen on TV since the year 2000! The changes of the 21st century were clear back in 2002 when Deanne Bray was cast as the lead actress in a television show called "Sue Thomas: F.B. Eye," (based on the real life of Sue Thomas, a deaf woman who worked for the FBI). That show was on from 2002-2005, and was the second highest rated show on the PAX network. In 2011, "Switched at Birth," was first shown on ABC Family. This program featured many Deaf actors and actresses, and a recurring role by Marlee Matlin. This was 25 years after Marlee won the Academy Award, confirming that Deaf actors are not a novelty, but equals in their field.

Deaf people are just as talented and skilled as their hearing counterparts. However, sadly, some people find this hard to believe. In 2012, I was watching Marlee Matlin doing an interview on a daytime talk show after her appearances on "Dancing with the Stars." A woman in the audience asked Marlee "When are you going to stop pretending to be Deaf?" Clearly, a lack of knowledge about deafness is still common, and it is things like this why I wrote this book.

While not all Deaf people are business professionals or actors, the workplace is not what it used to be for people who cannot hear. As I. King Jordan, the first Deaf President of Gallaudet University said, "Deaf people can do anything hearing people can do, except hear."

Part V

DEAF CHILDREN TODAY: A FUTURE WITHOUT A SOUND BARRIER

Note from Lois: *I began this book as a hearing child who suddenly became deaf at seven years of age. Throughout the book, I have written about the issues I have experienced and witnessed during my life as Deaf person. After we Deaf/HH broke the sound barrier, what deaf children will go through in their life now is much different than for me and deaf children of my generation.*

In Chapter 10, I offer some information and advice for hearing parents of deaf children today by giving some pros and cons of residential schools, mainstream schools, and cochlear implants, and emphasize the importance of hearing families communicating with their deaf child.

When I discuss children who do not hear, I use a little "d." The reason is deaf children have not yet developed their identity in life to either be Deaf or deaf.

"Communication is our greatest need. Given adequate means of free and easy communication, we can acquire language, and possibly speech as well."

Frederick C. Schreiber
Executive Director of the National Association of the Deaf (NAD) 1970

Chapter 10

HEARING PARENTS, DEAF CHILD

As I get to this last chapter of the book, I look back on having lived through so many changes and growth over my life, and the lives of millions of other Deaf/HH people, and I think "We had nothing, and now we have so much." When I first came up with the idea for writing a book, it was going to be some answering of questions many people had asked me about what it was like to be Deaf. But, mostly the book was going to be giving advice to hearing parents of a deaf child who had no resources—which is why this final chapter is the longest chapter in the book. However, between the time I first had the idea for a book, and now writing this last chapter, so much has changed. We have broken the sound barrier—and the issues facing hearing parents of deaf children today is quite different from when I first thought about writing a book. As I write this, I currently work with hearing parents of deaf children, have visited the California School for the Deaf in Fremont, California, and visited mainstream schools with deaf and hard of hearing programs. I do have some advice for hearing parents with deaf children—it is just different now than when I first had the idea for a book.

You have read in the last few chapters that with today's technologies, legislation, sign language interpreters, and job opportunities, there is very little that a Deaf or Hard of Hearing person with an education, family support, and determination cannot do. Go back and look at the amazing achievements of Helen Keller who was both deaf, *and* blind; Ms. Keller was a college graduate, an author of many books, a political activist, met several U.S. presidents, and had celebrity friends. She achieved all of these things over 100 years ago, long before *any* of the wonderful laws and technologies we have now! Although I lived most of my life in the "Dark Ages" before the benefit of today's "luxuries," I got an education, raised a family, held a job, earned a retirement pension, and own a home (I even wrote a book). Now, with all of the major changes that began in the mid-1990s, Deaf/HH people have so much more access and opportunities. Combined with a strong community and technology, many Deaf people do not consider themselves disabled. And why should they?

In the last chapter, I discussed the many new career opportunities available to those who are Deaf/HH, which means almost anything is possible for a deaf child now. But, there are still challenges for those who do not hear, and for parents of a deaf child. Even though the ADA was signed back in 1990, some people have never even heard of the ADA. Some may have heard of the ADA, but have no idea what the requirements are, or how to achieve the accommodations. This problem happens in doctor's offices, hospitals, schools, and more. Also, some public schools do not always follow the Individuals with Disabilities Education Act (IDEA). Therefore, parents of deaf children will still have to fight for their child's rights and access required by both the ADA and the IDEA.

If there is one point I must emphasize to hearing parents of a deaf child, even with the wonderful new technologies and laws, one fact has not changed: the time, effort, and choices parents make toward their deaf child's **language acquisition**, and **communicating with their child**, will greatly determine the child's outcome in life. My parents and siblings making the effort to communicate with me, and have me be part of the conversations, made me who I am today. Language acquisition and communication with family members makes all the difference in the world. Just like adults who hear that end up in the prison system, or with a dysfunctional life, their outcomes can usually be traced back to poor communication with their families, feeling unloved, and not getting the encouragement that they needed while growing up.

As human beings, we are social people. We all need to make connections and be part of a group or a community. A sense of belonging comes from a shared language. If you think about it, the reason most people socialize together is a shared language. Why do immigrants in this country try to find other immigrants from their home country? It is their shared language. Yes, it is their shared culture too, but a shared culture begins with having a shared language. If you ever read Mary Shelly's *Frankenstein*, you will remember that the monster just wanted someone to talk to, a friend, and a sense of belonging. The monster's anger came from a lack of connection. The only time the monster was able to have a conversation was with the blind man who did not judge the monster based on its looks. The blind man gave the monster a temporary sense of belonging and acceptance—based on a shared language.

Just as important as it is for a deaf child to acquire language, hearing parents of a deaf child must learn how to communicate with their child and support their child's language acquisition. While I would strongly suggest that hearing parents of a deaf child learn sign language along with their child learning sign language (because visual language is a deaf child's most natural way of learning language), it is not the *only* way to communicate. Even though as a child my family did not learn to sign (they did not have sign language classes or DVDs back in my day), they always made efforts to communicate with me, made me aware of what was going on or being said, and made me part of the family. Being included, and being part of the family conversations, makes all the difference.

So how does a deaf child acquire language? The same way that children who hear do. How do children who hear acquire language? Their parents interact with them, talk with them, have the child associate words with objects and actions, and learn from the television. But, how would a *deaf* child acquire language? Easy. Their parents would interact with them, sign with them, have the deaf child associate words with objects and actions, and learn from the television.

I have read that child development experts say that the critical language acquisition period is before the age of five. Many child development experts encourage parents of hearing babies (babies with perfect hearing and no family history of deafness) to teach their babies sign language before they can speak. Why do child development experts encourage the teaching of sign language? Because, they know that language acquisition and being able to communicate is very important for a child's development—early on, and later in life. They have also discovered that it greatly reduces frustration for babies because they can communicate their needs before they can talk, even as early as six months old. This is true for all babies, hearing or deaf.

Language acquisition is also very important later, as an adult. I believe if a person is deprived of language, they cannot learn to read, and will most likely be socially deprived, which very often leads to emotional problems, and they will most likely have financial troubles throughout their entire life. Yet, a well-known statistic in the Deaf community is that only about 12 percent of hearing parents with deaf children learn to sign with their deaf children. Sign language is the third most-used language in America, and the fourth most-studied. When I think about sign language being the fourth most-studied language in America, yet only about 12 percent of hearing parents with deaf children learn to sign, it makes me sad. Most of the people studying sign language are high school and college students, or adults who find sign language interesting—NOT hearing parents with deaf children.

There are plenty of DVDs, videos, flashcards, and books available that teach babies how to sign and build a vocabulary. There are many resources available on the Internet. One wonderful resource is "Signing Time." The series "Signing Time" is age-appropriate DVD's, charts, and lesson plans that teach babies, toddlers, and parents sign language. When a hearing parent learns sign language, whether from taking classes at a local community college or from a private tutor, it allows the hearing parent to interact with their deaf child, communicate with them, have their child associate signs with objects and actions, and create a bond with their child.

There is disagreement over whether a deaf child should learn sign language or the oral option only. I wrote about this in Chapter 3. There are people who support one method over the other (revisit both Chapter 3 and Chapter 4 on this point). I made it known to my readers that as a Deaf adult who learned sign language as a child, and struggled trying to learn how to read lips, that I support sign language first, and speech second, if speech is appropriate (remember, both speech, and learning how to read lips, is not possible for all deaf people. I had hearing and speech for seven years before I became deaf). What I support, and many other Deaf adults (who were once deaf children) support, is language acquisition—which leads to cognitive development. We believe it is more important to understand *the meanings of words*, than to try to learn how to form your lips and tongue to try to be able to *say or speak words*. Most of us who are Deaf believe that the meanings and concepts of words are best learned and understood visually, through sign language. We believe visual language is the most natural and easy form of language for a child that cannot hear, and after the meanings and concepts of words have been learned, speech can be practiced— if it is appropriate for that deaf child. A big mistake hearing parents can make is to think that "speaking" is the same as "language acquisition." Learning to form your lips and tongue to produce the sounds of words does not equal understanding the meanings and concepts of the words. The same goes for lip-reading. It is NOT language acquisition. Learning to read lips is a *skill*, a very difficult skill. About 30 percent of the English language is visible on the lips; therefore, about 70 percent is guesswork, lost, or misunderstood. I have developed the skill of lip-reading at a pretty good level, but I only get some of it, and always have to try my best to get the rest of it.

I was a child many years ago (more years ago than I would like to admit) and the decisions parents of deaf children must make are much greater today than what my parents had to make. Because of the new laws, the technology, and the different views on how to best educate a deaf child, parents must inform themselves about the choices they need to make—and learn that there will be choices that others will *want* parents of a deaf child to make. I am sad to say that with all the technology and laws, it often leads to financial motivations for some in the field of working with deaf and hard of hearing children, and some of the "advice" given to parents is not what is best for the child, but what is best for the advice giver's wallet. It is sad, but true.

When I was a child, there was not a "Get a cochlear implant, or not get a cochlear implant?" decision for my parents to make, and there was not a "Mainstream School, or Deaf Residential School?" decision for my parents to make either. Part of what is causing confusion for hearing parents of a deaf child is that there are several views on deafness. Deafness is viewed from three perspectives in our society, **medical**, **functional**, and **cultural**:

> **Medical**: The medical perspective is the idea that deafness is an abnormal *health* condition that must be "treated"

or "fixed." It is viewing deafness by measurement of decibel loss and frequency loss, focusing only on the ears' ability to process sounds. It is the usual view of many medical doctors and audiologists. The recommendation for "treatment" is to try to make a deaf person as "close to being able to hear" as possible, or be "normal," as they perceive "normal" to be.

Functional: The functional perspective is a comparison. It is a comparison of "How well does a deaf person function as close to, or like, a hearing person." The functional perspective is sometimes found in statements such as "He/She is deaf, but their work is just as good as all the other employees."

Cultural: (I discussed this in Chapter 4 with the little "d" or big "D" in deaf/Deaf) The cultural perspective is the way in which Deaf individuals identify and view themselves *culturally*, not the measurement of their hearing loss. A culturally Deaf person embraces the traditions, values, language, norms, and long history of people who are Deaf. Culturally Deaf people do not view themselves as disabled, but rather, as a part of a cultural and language minority. A person who has hearing loss, but associates with the traditions, values, language, and norms of those who hear and speak, is not culturally Deaf.

As you might imagine, these different perspectives often lead to disagreements. I believe that when hearing parents are seeking advice about their deaf child, it is very important that they think about which perspective the advice giver has. Many of us in the Deaf community say, "Do not bow down to the white coat." That is because people in white coats mostly give the *medical* perspective, and do not know everything about what it is to be Deaf, live as a Deaf person, or be a parent of a child that is deaf or hard of hearing. It is not my intention to put doctors down; however, most medical schools do not teach students about the wonderful and rich lives of Deaf people—only the medical causes of hearing loss (maybe reading this book will help them).

Every parent wants a healthy, "normal" baby. Often, when hearing parents find out their child is deaf, it feels devastating. Unfortunately, those holding a medical perspective of deafness are usually a hearing parent's first contact, and they confirm the hearing parent's fears and uncomfortable feelings. However, the fears are not necessary. Deaf children *can* and *do* grow and develop just like children with normal hearing—and the last few chapters of this book show that! Hearing parents of a deaf/hh child just need to learn about deafness. I strongly believe they should meet Deaf/HH adults who were once deaf/hh children, and meet hearing parents that raised deaf/ hh children. I highly recommend that hearing parents with deaf children go to Deaf/ HH service agencies, schools that specialize in deaf/hh education programs, and read books about deafness. I also recommend downloading the Parent Resource Guide from the California Department of Education, and doing some research on the Internet. Parents need to know that everything will be okay.

Some interesting information: back in 2010, a new bill was introduced in California, known as AB 2072. This bill would require handing out information to parents of newly identified babies with hearing loss. The original draft of the bill was very one-sided; the information to be given to the new parents of deaf or hard of hearing babies was only to come from audiologists—most of whom knew nothing about deafness and language acquisition—only the *medical* view of decibel loss and speech therapy. Many of those involved in drafting and supporting AB 2072 had financial motives. The Academy of Audiologists and the AG Bell Association were a big part of this movement. The proposed bill was little more than just advertising cochlear implants and private schools—that tried to make a deaf child "close to being able to hear." The information they wanted handed out was mostly "treatment options," and they had lobbyists and financial investors to persuade legislators to help pass AB 2072. However, Deaf leaders from Northern and Southern California, and local members of the Deaf community banded together in Sacramento and fought to have AB 2072 amended. Deaf leaders and members of the Deaf community wanted full information to be handed out—meaning, having all information known to new parents about language acquisition, deaf education options, and sign language —not just the medical perspective and the oral option only. Our Deaf leaders and the Deaf community wanted the State of California to publish and distribute the informational packets handed out to parents of newly identified deaf and hard of hearing babies—to remove all profit motives for what information went inside the informational packets. Deaf leaders and the Deaf community wanted to amend AB 2072 to require putting together an advisory panel to help write the information going in the information packets. With the heartfelt motto, "Nothing about us without us," Deaf leaders and the Deaf community wanted a balanced advisory panel to include adults who were Deaf/HH and used ASL; teachers of the Deaf who used ASL; a parent of a deaf child that used ASL; and a researcher involved in the study of sign language. Who better to ask than Deaf adults who have experienced being a deaf child? Who better to know about all the perspectives of deafness than members of the Deaf Community? The Academy of Audiologists and the AG Bell Association did not want AB 2072 to be amended to include all this balanced information. They actually ended up lobbying against their own bill! It never made it to Governor Arnold Schwarzenegger's desk. (As I wrote about at the end of Chapter 3, leaders of the California Association of the Deaf, NorCal Services for Deaf and Hard of Hearing, and the California Coalition of Options Schools joined together here in Sacramento in 2015 to pass SB210, focusing on the bigger problem of deaf kids arriving at kindergarten language deprived and language delayed. This is very encouraging.)

Cochlear implants were the main issue of AB 2072. One concern that parents of a deaf or hard of hearing child face today is whether to get cochlear implants for their child. This is a very controversial topic because of the different perspectives on deafness. I am not an expert, and I would only tell any person considering a cochlear implant (parents of a deaf/ hh child, or a Deaf adult) to gather all the information they can, and make an educated decision. I would also remind them that there is a financial motive for many who recommend getting cochlear implants.

Again, I am not an expert on cochlear implants. Part of my experience is what I have been told by my Deaf friends who have received them, or a few parents that I have met whose children have received them, or what I have seen when I have gone into some mainstream schools with a deaf and hard of hearing program. When I visit some mainstream schools with deaf/ hh students, I see children with cochlear implants. Most of them can just hear some sounds and understand just a few words of spoken language. They continue to use sign language, and still have to use interpreters. However, I have seen a few children who stopped going to special education classes after receiving their cochlear implants, and went into public schools with children who had normal hearing. For those kids, yes, the cochlear implants were totally helpful. But, a cochlear implant will not "turn a deaf person into a hearing person," which is why many people with cochlear implants still continue to use sign language. I do know that many children that have a cochlear implant miss the side conversations of the other kids, because they cannot hear past a certain range, or can only focus on one person at a time. They often miss what others in the room are saying. While it may seem silly, hearing side conversations and hearing gossip is a big part of learning and social development.

I have one adult friend who absolutely loves his cochlear implant, and is very glad he had the surgery (he lost his hearing at 17). I have another adult friend who said her implant is "Okay, but if I had to do it over again, I would not do it." I have another adult friend who has completely stopped using her cochlear implant.

I would never tell a parent of a deaf/ hh child what to do, or not to do, about cochlear implants. However, I can offer some facts to consider:

- A cochlear implant will not give a deaf/ hh person normal hearing, or turn them into a "hearing person"
- Cochlear implants do help some deaf and hard of hearing people
- Some individuals cannot be helped at all by a cochlear implant
- Some lives are improved because of cochlear implants; however, some lives are made worse
- There is a very large amount of therapy and work involved with learning how to "hear" with a cochlear implant after the surgery
- There are several risks to a cochlear implant, including facial paralysis

- There can be side effects from a cochlear implant such as vertigo, tinnitus, and nerve damage to the tongue and taste buds
- There has been millions of dollars paid out in lawsuits against makers of cochlear implants

I have met people who all have different experiences with their cochlear implants; although, I have never seen a deaf person "become a hearing person" because of their cochlear implant surgery. I do not mean a person who had hearing and speech all their lives, lost their hearing, received a cochlear implant at 50 years of age, had much of their hearing restored, and got their life back close to how they once knew it. That is *very* uncommon. In my experience, I have only seen Deaf people who have a cochlear implant, but still must use sign language interpreters for staff meetings at work, sign language interpreters in their college classes, and sign language interpreters to voice for them in presentations and interviews. My son and his wife are certified interpreters, and many of their clients are people who have cochlear implants, but still need to use sign language interpreting services.

When many of us in the Deaf community talk about cochlear implants, we often say, "Still deaf." We say this because we all know that when the implants come off at bedtime, or do not work some reason, that person is completely deaf. There have been situations where something happened with a cochlear implant and it caused a big problem. I personally know about one incident, because I was a private tutor for a young deaf girl named Katie and her hearing parents. Katie had a cochlear implant and went to a mainstream school. She and her parents did not know sign language. One Friday night, her cochlear implant broke. Her mother was not able to get her daughter in to see the audiologist until Monday. Because nobody knew sign language, the family had to communicate through text messages. Katie was only six years old at the time, and her reading skills were not well-developed. Katie could talk to her parents, but she could not hear what they were saying back to her. They all had to try to communicate through texting and gesturing for the whole weekend. On Monday morning, they could not send Katie to school because Katie could not hear or communicate with the teacher and the other students. This was a scary experience for Katie's parents. They were referred to me because I taught sign language and did private tutoring. I worked with that family for almost two years, and all three of them became good at signing. Katie's father eventually got a job out of state, and I have since lost touch with them. But, I do know that they were grateful that they could now communicate with each other by both signing and speaking.

Again, cochlear implants can help some people, and they are the right choice for some. One of the issues for deaf children is that the critical language acquisition period is before the age of five. Deaf children, who do not acquire language, then get a cochlear implant at five or six, will be behind in their language development. A cochlear implant cannot erase all the lost time. There is also a training period, working with audiologists, and speech therapists, for the child to learn how to train the brain to process sounds that they have never heard before, and to learn how to pronounce words. The period after getting cochlear implants is not easy. An important thing to know is even those who sell cochlear implants say that the best candidates for cochlear implants are people who "already had speech and language development first." Yes, language acquisition *is* the most important thing of all.

Another decision that parents of a deaf child face today is what kind of school they should send their child to— a mainstream school, or a residential school for the deaf.

At residential schools, students live on campus during the week and then go home on the weekends, holidays, and for the summer (unless they live near a residential school and can come home every night). All of the students in residential schools are deaf/hh. Mainstream schools are regular schools for kids with normal hearing, but often have a deaf education program or a special needs program—but not always.

Because I went to a residential school, my heart will always be with residential schools. However, some mainstream schools can be very good. When I interviewed people for this section of the book, I found that there is no easy answer to "Which kind of school is better?" I interviewed some hearing parents of deaf children and asked them how they decided what the best choice was for their child. I met with Deaf parents who favored mainstream schools. I met with other Deaf parents who would only send their deaf child to a residential school. I spoke with Deaf/HH adults who attended both mainstream and residential schools as children, and they had mixed feelings about both types of schools. I believe when parents of a deaf child decide what type of school to send their child to, they should think about their child individually and ask, "What is the best choice for *my* deaf child, not all deaf children?" Their decision may also be affected by where the parents live, or what is available in their area.

When I was growing up, a residential school was the main option for parents finding formal education for their deaf child. Placing deaf children in mainstream schools did not begin until the late 1970s, more in the 1980s and 1990s, and then even more in the 2000s. Because there are less residential schools in the US, most hearing parents are told about mainstream school options first. Mainstream schools can be good—the ones that have a deaf and hard of hearing program, have administrators that understand deafness and the learning needs and styles of a deaf student, and have some Deaf teachers and staff members. However, not many mainstream schools have all this. What many mainstream schools do have is a "special needs" or "special education" department, where they put all the kids together in the same class. Are the educational needs of a 14-year-old student on the autism spectrum the same as a nine-year-old student who is deaf, or an 11-year-old student who uses a wheelchair? Mainstream schools can provide deaf children exposure and interaction with the mainstream (most people hear), and this can be good for a deaf child's social development and learning the norms of hearing people and popular culture. Unfortunately, what often happens in mainstream schools is that the deaf student is the *only* deaf student in the entire school, and is isolated and ignored. Something that a parent of a deaf child told me was that they made sure there were several other deaf children at the mainstream school before enrolling their child. If a deaf child were going to be the only deaf student at their school, they suggested the child go to a residential school. In this case, a residential school would be better for social development, because the residential school will be full of peers and adults who share the same language and culture.

The Rehabilitation Act of 1973 calls for the "least restrictive environment in education," which many school administrators believe is just putting a deaf student in a classroom with hearing students and giving them an interpreter. This one-size-fits-all approach is not appropriate for all deaf/hh students. What often happens in these "least restrictive environments" is that there are no Deaf staff members, nobody in the school knows sign language (or knows very little), there is only one deaf student in the entire school, and sometimes there is not even an interpreter provided for the deaf student. Often, the first job a beginning interpreter gets is in a K-8 school. Often, these inexperienced interpreters receive no supervision because the administrators do not know sign language, and cannot tell if the interpreter is good or bad (although, this has improved as some states are only hiring interpreters with certification). When a deaf student is the only deaf person in the school, they stay with the interpreter all day, and take recess and lunch with the interpreter. So, this one adult is not only the interpreter, but also becomes a language model, a role model, and a best friend. With no supervision, that interpreter may be bad at all four. Again, some mainstream schools can be very good. But what I describe here, I have witnessed when I visited mainstream schools, and parents must do their homework before deciding what school and accommodations are best for their deaf child.

Residential schools can be another option. One of the main advantages of a residential school is that students become fluent in sign language. Again, most Deaf adults believe that language acquisition for deaf children is best developed visually, through sign language. Having almost all Deaf teachers and Deaf staff at a residential school, and being with other students who are all deaf/hh too, the exposure to sign language is much more than what a deaf child could ever get at a mainstream school. Residential schools also have student clubs and student organizations that a deaf student would rarely be a part of in a mainstream school. The same goes for sports. Deaf students rarely go out for any sport, or make the team, in a mainstream school. If a child is the only deaf student in a mainstream school, then a residential school would be a better option for language development, social development, athletic skill development, having a sense of belonging, and building their self-esteem. While deaf students in mainstream schools often form friendships with hearing students, and often develop a sense of belonging and self-esteem, it is different from residential schools. Still, many parents do not like the idea of sending their young children off to residential school (if they do not live near a residential school). One reason why many parents choose a mainstream school for their deaf child is that there are no residential schools within hundreds of miles, and they want to keep their child close.

Some parents are told that residential schools may not be as challenging as mainstream schools. This is because the focus of the curriculum is different in mainstream and residential schools. Some parents are told that a deaf student is more likely to develop better fluency in English at a mainstream school, as ASL is not English. However, there is no guarantee that a deaf student will develop better fluency in English at a mainstream school, as deaf children often struggle to develop English fluency in mainstream schools too. Inexperienced interpreters, and administrators in mainstream schools that do not understand a deaf student's educational needs and learning styles, can prevent a deaf student from getting the most out their education in *all* subjects, not just English. I do not disagree that if a deaf student develops better fluency in English, and has friendships with other kids who hear, they have greater exposure to the mainstream and will learn the norms of hearing people. But, Deaf teachers and Deaf role models in residential schools can be very important for a deaf child's personal development.

When I asked some young Deaf/HH adults who had experienced both mainstream and residential schools, they told me that each school had their advantages, and that spending some time in both types of schools gave them a feeling of being well-rounded. It is not a bad idea for a deaf child to experience both types of schools, and some parents actually do choose both types of schools to see what works best.

What I have mostly seen is that Deaf parents with deaf children will send their kids to a residential school. However, some Deaf parents I interviewed preferred mainstream schools to a residential school. If a mainstream school does have a deaf and hard of hearing program, has other deaf students, and has some Deaf faculty members, Deaf parents sometimes choose that mainstream school.

Like many others I discussed this topic with, I believe if there are no other deaf students at the mainstream school, and the child lives in a home where the hearing parents and family members do not sign and communicate with them, the deaf child's loneliness and isolation will be damaging. In those situations, attending a residential school would be better for a deaf child's personal development and language acquisition.

But, it will not be a fix-all answer. If the child comes home on the weekends, and none of the hearing family signs and communicates with the deaf child, he or she will become withdrawn. Neither a residential school, nor a mainstream school, can erase the loss and damage from a lack of communication with parents and siblings (remember my earlier example from Mary Shelly's *Frankenstein*).

Whatever education decisions parents make, what a deaf child needs most is a sense of belonging, and knowing that they are loved. Most of the successful Deaf and Hard of Hearing adults that I described in Chapter 9 have a few things in common: language acquisition, love, and encouragement. Here are two short stories from some hearing parents of deaf children, whom I interviewed:

Interview 1:

I first met Phyllis and her husband Bill (both hearing) when their two deaf children (Renee and Eric) were 7 and 5 years old. Both children were born deaf. I could see right away that both Rene and Eric were happy and intelligent children. Every once in a while, I would see Phyllis and Bill and their kids at Deaf community events through the years. It was actually many years later, for this book, when Phyllis told me a story. She told me how when Renee was little, she was an unusually beautiful girl with big blue eyes and blonde curly hair. All the neighborhood children were fascinated with her. Not only by her beauty, but also the fact that she could not hear or talk. They wanted to play with Renee, but did not know how to communicate with her. Phyllis told the neighborhood children "If you want to play with this beautiful girl and her brother, you need to learn sign language first. Then you can come and play with them." Sure enough, the neighborhood kids flocked to Phyllis's house to learn how to communicate in sign language. Phyllis taught all the neighbor kids basic signs so they could communicate with Renee and Eric. Phyllis told me that she and Bill chose a mainstream school for Renee and Eric because the school had four other deaf children who signed. When Phyllis and Bill checked into the mainstream school, they felt comfortable with the staff and interpreters and the services provided by the school for the four other deaf children. Phyllis and Bill attended Deaf events and Deaf functions with their kids while they were growing up, which is how I would run into them from time to time. During our interview, I learned that Renee and her brother both graduated from a 4-year university (they attended different universities). Renee became a child psychologist, and works with deaf children of hearing parents. Eric went into Engineering.

Interview 2:

Pat told me that she was so scared when she found out she had a deaf child. She worried that her child could never grow up to be independent and successful. But over time, education and understanding later changed her feelings. Pat began with having the whole family learn sign language, as well as getting involved in giving her son the best possible education. They chose to send their son, Timmy, to a residential school. Pat and her husband attended Deaf community events, as well as becoming familiar with other hearing parents who also signed. When Timmy came home on the weekends, she and her husband were able to communicate with him. Timmy was always made to feel loved and a part of the family. Timmy graduated from Gallaudet University and is now a math teacher, teaching both hearing and deaf children at a public mainstream school (he uses a full-time interpreter for the hearing children). Timmy married his classmate, and has three hearing children who all sign.

I wish there were more hearing parents of deaf children like these. These are hearing parents who made the difference in their deaf children's lives by communicating with them and giving them a sense of belonging. Sadly, this is not always the case. The following story shows the opposite of Phyllis, Bill, and Pat. It's a story told to me by a counselor that worked in a juvenile detention center.

Interview 3:

Robert and Ronnie were born deaf to parents who hear. Both parents were deeply angered to have deaf children. Robert and Ronnie's parents often complained about the misery that God had burdened them with by giving them deaf children. At no point did they try to learn about deafness, or to learn how to communicate with their deaf children. Because Robert and Ronnie's parents never learned to communicate with them, these children did not acquire language. Fortunately, both kids were sent to a residential school. They were exposed to language for the first time when they were six and seven years old (think just how far behind these little boys were in their language acquisition). By this time, Robert and Ronnie were both already "educationally delayed" and showed behavior problems. Their parents sent them to the residential school because the school took care of the kids nine months out of the year (today, residential school children go home every weekend). The three months of summer when they went home, their parents "tolerated" Robert and Ronnie. By now, these two brothers had learned sign language and could communicate with each other. The brothers could not communicate with their parents or anybody else in the family, or in their neighborhood, so they just stayed with each other all the time. The juvenile detention center counselor told me that Robert and Ronnie had low social development, and that they were in and out of Juvenile Hall for years—not always both at once, but both of them at different times. When they became adults, both Robert and Ronnie spent time in jail for drug offenses. The last time she had heard from them, Robert was in prison, and Ronnie was unemployed and living on Social Security.

Yes, Robert and Ronnie's story also happens to hearing children who come from families where they are not loved and supported too. However, I believe the difference between Renee, Eric, Timmy, and Robert and Ronnie began with whether or not their parents learned to communicate with them.

In my own personal experience, I became deaf at seven, and I remember my family did their best to restore "normalcy" as soon as possible. My older brothers were told to tell me about the sounds, and always include me in all conversations. My brothers were reminded to look at me and tell me what they or my other siblings said. I was always told to look at a person when they were talking, so I would be included in everything with my family. Even if I did not understand the conversations, I always felt equal and important.

My father bought all my brothers bicycles at one time or another, and I remember the day that my father said that I could also have one. My brothers rode around being "tough"—by skidding, and jumping off ramps. I would tag along trying to be tough, too. One of their stunts was to climb a hill on a dirt road, then ride back down real fast, and skid around the curve near the bottom. The faster they could make it through the curve, the more everyone cheered. Wanting to accomplish the feat myself, I huffed and puffed with my bicycle to the top of the hill, gathered up my courage, and peddled down as fast as I could. But, when I got to the curve, I was so scared, and I closed my eyes, thinking I could somehow make it without looking. When I opened my eyes, I was lying on the ground with a deep bloody gash in my cheek. One of my brothers rushed me to the doctor's office down the street. My other brothers went to get my father. Sitting in the doctor's office getting stitches, I did not cry—until I saw my father entering the office. He seemed angry and worried. Even though I could no longer hear his voice, I could see his anger. He was pacing about, and bawling out my brothers who sat silent with their eyes down to the floor. My bicycle clearly was ready for the city dump, and my bicycle days were over. Wrong! Once I healed, my father took me to the store and let me pick out a new bike. Imagine what this did for my self-esteem and confidence! It told me that it was okay to fall down, get back up, brush myself off, and try again—even if I was deaf. My parents in no way let my deafness prevent me from being equal to everybody who hears.

The bicycle incident was not the only time my father encouraged my self-esteem. When my brothers tried to teach me to play baseball, I stupidly stood watching right behind the brother with the bat. Of course, I was accidentally hit in the head with the bat because I was standing too close. I was knocked out cold, and I awoke lying on the couch with an ice pack on my big bump. My mother and father were bending over me, worried and talking back and forth with my brothers. I thought, *"Probably the end of my baseball games now."* No way! Two days later, I was right back on the diamond. Only this time, my father was there to watch me, making my brother show me where to stand and making sure I stayed the proper distance away from the bat.

It was not until I was older that I realized why I grew up to have such confidence in myself, and how I developed such a positive attitude. Years ago, I was talking to my Deaf friend Edwin about my childhood. He looked at me and said in sign, "You were born into a royal family!" He then told me how neither of his parents ever communicated with him. He went on to tell me all about his resentment that he carried all his life about this, and that he still has bitterness today. Edwin told me that because of this, he had very little contact with his hearing parents throughout his life.

After that conversation, I started to ask other Deaf people if they had a happy childhood with their hearing parents. I am sad to say that most of them said, "No," and mostly spoke of unhappy childhoods because their hearing parents and siblings never really communicated with them. Most of them felt closer to their Deaf friends at residential school than to their own blood families. I was told many different stories about how they never knew what was going on in and around their family, and that they never had communication with their family members when they were around them. I was told of many instances where parents and other hearing people at family gatherings talked happily among themselves while the deaf child or Deaf adult was left alone and feeling isolated. The sad part is that, like Edwin, these Deaf individuals no longer care to visit their hearing families. Rather, they created their own family within the Deaf culture where they were accepted, and could communicate and socialize in a shared language. They found happiness in the world where their peers often told each other "I love you," and hugged each other to show they care—in the world where the little "d" in deaf becomes the big "D" in Deaf.

One last story about a little deaf girl named Dawn. Back in the early 1980s, when I worked at NorCal Center on Deafness as a Community Education Specialist, my job was to educate the public about deafness, and make the public aware of our agency and our services. One day, a couple with a little deaf girl named Dawn came to our agency to get help.

They wanted some guidance on how to get their little three year-old girl to learn to lip-read and speak, on the recommendation of their doctor. At the time, Dawn had no language. I told the parents in a very direct way, "Forget about your deaf child learning to lip-read and speak; teach her sign language, and communicate with her." Both parents were stunned, and looked at me and said, "We do not know how to do sign language." I told them to come to our center twice a week and I would teach them how to sign and communicate with this beautiful little blonde-haired child. They were both shocked, but fortunately, they agreed. I worked with this family for several months until they had enough sign vocabulary to communicate, and to teach Dawn. Dawn was a sweet little girl whose face would light up every time her parents brought her to the center. After a few years, I lost contact with the family.

About 30 years had passed when an interpreter friend of mine told me that she wanted to take me to lunch to meet "someone." My first reaction was that she wanted me to meet a man. However, she told me that this person is not a man, but a woman. I got to the restaurant early and waited for my friend to bring this "someone" to meet me. My friend arrived, with a lovely blonde-haired Deaf woman that I did not know. This woman was so excited to see me, and the first words to me were "Thank you for saving my life!" *Saving her life? I have never done CPR!* I felt embarrassed, but told her in all honesty, "I am sorry, but I do not know who you are." She laughed a bit and began to talk about the past. She told me that her parents came to see me when she was little, and from then on, her parents signed, and were very much involved with her life. She said if she were forced into lip-reading and trying to speak, she would have been very unhappy. But, because her parents signed to her, and for her, and showed their love and support, she led a very happy life. So, in her own choice of words, I "saved her life."

Naturally, I was very touched by this incident. To be able to have such an impact on someone, and "save their life," is a meaningful reward. It is my hope and dream that parents, students, or whoever reads this book, can also be helped, and maybe many lives can be "saved" by this simple guidance written here.

I have run into Dawn a few times since that meeting. What is interesting is that Dawn has three deaf children herself, and she prefers a mainstream school over a residential school for her kids. I told her that I prefer residential schools. But, what we do agree on is that language acquisition, and hearing parents communicating with their deaf child, are the two most important influences on the outcome of a deaf child's life.

My conclusion in this final chapter is that there is not one simple answer for a school choice or cochlear implant for a deaf child today; but, I would advise parents to gather all the information you can to help decide which is best for *your* child. But above all, communicate with your child!

Afterword

If you are reading this, I can only assume you have made it this far. I hope the information in this book has helped you to better understand deafness. As our conversation comes to a close, my hope is that my life-long dreams have been realized: that I have left this world a better place than I found it, and that I have been a part of changing how Deaf people are viewed in this world. With that, I bid you farewell.

References

Chapman-Martin, Talia
Cruz, Jessica
Egbert, John
*Fair, Sara Jane
Farinha, Sheri
Piscitelli, Stephanie
Wilson, Marlowe

These are some individuals with whom I did personal interviews to gather information for some of the chapters. Other personal interviews were done with an agreement of confidentiality, and their names were changed as they appeared throughout this book.

*I have never met Sara Jane Fair personally, and we do not know each other. I saw an article that she wrote online. I did not quote her. However, I did incorporate a point in Chapter 10 that she made in an online article.